Building the
Data Warehouse

Books from QED

Database

Building the Data Warehouse
Migrating to DB2
DB2: The Complete Guide to Implementation
    and Use
DB2 Design Review Guidelines
DB2: Maximizing Performance of Online
    Production Systems
Embedded SQL for DB2
SQL for DB2 and SQL/DS Application
    Developers
Database Management Systems
IBM's Repository Manager/MVS
How to Use ORACLE SQL*PLUS
ORACLE: Building High Performance Online
    Systems
ORACLE Design Review Guidelines
Developing Client/Server Applications in an
    Architected Environment

Systems Engineering

On Time, Within Budget: Software Project
    Management Practices and Techniques
Information Systems Architecture:
    Development in the 90's
Quality Assurance for Information Systems
User-Interface Design Techniques for Software
    Developers: Workstations, PC's, Mainframes
Managing Software Projects
The Complete Guide to Software Testing
A Structured Approach to Systems Testing
Rapid Application Prototyping
The Software Factory
Data Architecture: The Information Paradigm
Software Engineering with Formal Metrics

Management

Introduction to Data Security and Controls
How to Automate Your Computer Center
Controlling the Future
The UNIX Industry
Ethical Conflicts in Information and Computer
    Science, Technology, and Business
Mind Your Business

IBM Mainframe Series

From Mainframe to Workstations: Offloading
    Application Development
CICS/VS: A Guide to Application Debugging
CICS Application and System Programming
CICS: A Guide To Performance Tuning
MVS COBOL II Power Programmer's Desk
    Reference
VSE JCL and Subroutines for Application
    Programmers
VSE COBOL II Power Programmer's Desk
    Reference
Introduction to CSP
CSP Version 3.3 Application Development
The MVS Primer
VSAM for the Application Programmer
TSO/E CLISTs: The Complete Tutorial and
    Desk Reference
CICS for COBOL Programmers
QMF: How to Use Query Management Facility
    with DB2 and SQL/DS
DOS/VSE: Introduction to the Operating
    System
DOS/VSE JCL: Mastering Job Control
    Language
DOS/VSE: CICS Systems Programming
VSAM: Guide to Optimization and Design
MVS/JCL: Mastering Job Control Language
MVS/TSO: Mastering CLISTs
MVS/TSO: Mastering Native Mode and ISPF
REXX in the TSO Environment, 2nd Edition

Technical

C Language for Programmers
VAX/VMS: Mastering DCL Commands and
    Utilities
The PC Data Handbook
UNIX C Shell Desk Reference
Designing and Implementing Ethernet Networks
The Handbook for Microcomputer Technicians
Open Systems

Building the
Data Warehouse

W.H. Inmon

QED Technical Publishing Group
Boston • Toronto • London

© 1992 QED Information Sciences, Inc.
P.O. Box 82-181
Wellesley, MA 02181

QED Technical Publishing Group is a division of QED Information Sciences, Inc.

Library of Congress Catalog Number: 91-41284
International Standard Book Number: 0-89435-404-3

Printed in the United States of America

92 93 94 10 9 8 7 6 5 4 3 2

Library of Congress Cataloging-in-Publication Data
Inmon, William H.
  Building the data warehouse / W.H. Inmon.
  284 p.   22.86 cm.
  Includes bibliographical references and index.
  ISBN 0-89435-404-3
  1. Data base management.   I. Title.
QA76.9.D3I5372   1992
005.74--dc20   91-41284
                                                CIP

For Jeanne Friedman,
a friend for all times

Contents

Preface

Databases and database theory have been around for a long time. Early renditions of databases centered around serving every purpose known to the information processing community—from transaction to batch processing to analytical processing. In most cases, the primary focus of the early database systems was operational—usually transactional—processing. In recent years, a more sophisticated notion of database has emerged—one that serves operational needs and another to serve informational or analytical needs. To some extent, this more enlightened notion of database is due to the advent of PC's, 4gl technology, and the empowerment of the end user.

The split of operational and informational databases occurs for many reasons.

- The data serving operational needs are physically different data from those serving informational or analytic needs.
- The supporting technology for operational processing is fundamentally different from the technology used to support informational or analytical needs.
- The user community of operational data is different from the one served by informational or analytical data.

- The processing characteristics for the operational environment and the informational environment are fundamentally different.

Because of these reasons, the modern way to build systems is to separate operational and informational or analytical processing and data.

This book is about the analytical (or the DSS) environment and the structuring of data in that environment. The focus of the book is on what is termed the "data warehouse," which is at the heart of informational, DSS processing.

The discussions in this book are geared toward the manager and the developer. Where appropriate, some level of discussion will be at the technical level. But for the most part, the book is about issues and technique. This book is meant to serve as a guideline for the designer and the developer.

What is analytical, informational processing? It is processing that serves the needs of management in the decision-making process. Often known as DSS (decision support systems) processing, analytical processing looks across broad vistas of data to detect trends. Instead of looking at one or two records of data (as is the case in operational processing), when the DSS analyst does analytical processing, many records are accessed.

In addition, it is very rare for the DSS analyst to update data. In operational systems, data are constantly being updated at the individual record level. In analytical processing, records are constantly being accessed, and their contents are gathered for analysis, but little or no alteration of individual records occurs.

In analytical processing, the response time requirements are greatly relaxed compared to those of traditional operational processing. Analytical response time is measured from 30 minutes to 24 hours. Response times measured in this range for operational processing would be an unmitigated disaster.

The network that serves the analytical community is a much smaller one than the one that serves the operational community. Usually there are fewer users of the analytical network than of the operational network.

Unlike the technology that serves the analytical environment, operational environment technology must concern itself with data and transaction locking, contention for data, deadlock, etc.

There are then many major differences between the operational environment and the analytical environment. This book is about the analytical, DSS environment and addresses the following issues:

- granularity of data
- partitioning of data
- metadata
- lack of credibility of data
- integration of DSS data
- the time basis of DSS data
- identifying the source of DSS data—the system of record
- migration and methodology

This book is for developers, managers, designers, data administrators, database administrators, and others who are building systems in a modern data processing environment. In addition, students of information processing will find this book useful.

There are many people who have contributed—directly and indirectly—to this effort. The following list only reflects a few contributors.

- Sue Osterfelt, Storage Tek
- Claudia Imhoff, GE Consulting
- John Zachman, independent consultant
- Jim Kerr, Equitable Insurance
- Ed Young, Amdahl Corporation
- Mike Schmidt, Rolm Corporation
- Jim Ashbrook, Prism Solutions
- Cynthia Schmidt, Prism Solutions
- Peter LaPorte, Tandem Corporation
- John Viescas, Tandem Corporation
- George Coleman, Teradata Corporation
- Paul Hessinger, independent consultant
- Jeanne Friedman, CCA
- Cheryl Estep, Chevron Corporation
- Nancy Ryan, Storage Tek

1

Evolution of Decision Support Systems

The world of information systems is an "immature" world. One has to be careful in using that word in public because it normally has a negative connotation. But from a historical perspective it is true. When you compare the history of information processing to that of other professions, there is no contest. We are told that the hieroglyphics in Egypt are primarily the work of an accountant declaring how much grain is owed the pharoah. We walk down the streets of Rome on paths and structures laid out by a civil engineer over 2,000 years ago. Other professions have roots back to antiquity.

So, the information processing profession is immature because it has existed only since the early 1960s.

One of the manifestations of the information processing profession's youth is the insistence on dwelling on detail. There is the notion that if we get the details right, the end result will somehow take care of itself and we will achieve success. It's like saying that if we know how to lay concrete, how to drill, and how to install nuts and bolts, we don't have to worry about the shape or the use of the structure we are building. Such an attitude would drive a more mature civil engineer crazy.

The story of the data warehouse begins with an evolution in which the larger forces at work in the industry are considered. The larger architecture that is being carved out—of which the data warehouse is the focal piece—is best viewed from a broad, not a detailed, perspective.

THE EVOLUTION

It is interesting that DSS processing is at the end of a long and complex evolution but continues to evolve. The origins of DSS processing hark back to the very early days of computers.

Figure 1.1 shows the evolution of processing from the early 1960s up to 1980.

In the early 1960s, the world of computation consisted of creating individual applications that were run on master files. The applications featured reports and programs, usually COBOL. Punched cards were common. The master files were stored on magnetic tape files, which were good for storing a large volume of data cheaply but had the drawback of needing to be accessed sequentially. Indeed, it is often said that in a given pass of a magnetic tape file where 100 percent of the records have to be accessed, only 5 percent or fewer of the records were actually needed. In addition, accessing an entire tape file may take as long as 20 to 30 minutes, depending on the data on the file and the processing that is being done.

Around the mid-1960s, the growth of master files and magnetic tape exploded. Soon there were master files everywhere. And with that growth came huge amounts of redundant data everywhere. The proliferation of master files and massive redundancy of data presented some very insidious problems.

- the need to synchronize data upon update
- the complexity of maintenance of programs
- the complexity of developing new programs
- the amount of hardware required to support all the master files

In short order, the problems of master files that were inherent to the medium itself became stifling. It is an interesting conjecture to speculate what the world of information processing would look like if the only medium for storing data had been the magnetic tape.

If there never had been anything to store bulk data on other

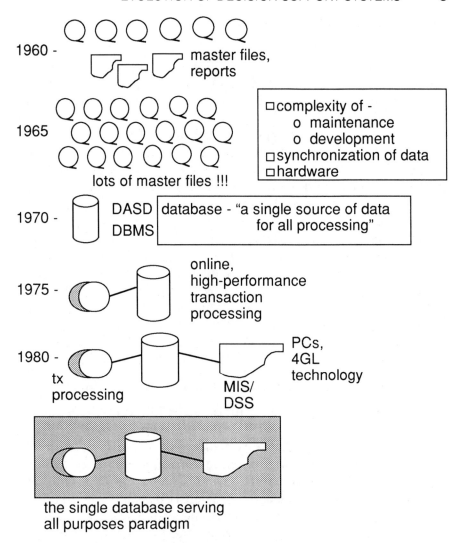

Figure 1.1.   The early evolutionary stages of the architected environment.

than magnetic tape files, the world would have never had large, fast reservations systems, ATM systems, and the like. Indeed, the ability to store and manage data on a variety of media other than magnetic tape files opened up the way for processing that brought the technician and the businessperson together.

THE ADVENT OF DASD

By 1970, the day of a new technology for the storage and access of data had dawned. The 1970s saw the advent of disk storage, or DASD (direct access storage device). Disk storage was fundamentally different from magnetic tape storage in that data could be accessed directly on DASD. There was no need to go through records 1, 2, 3, ... n to get to record n + 1. Once the address of record n + 1 was known, it was a simple matter to go to record n + 1 directly. Furthermore, the time required to go to record n + 1 was significantly less than the time required to scan a tape. In fact, the time to locate a record on DASD was measured in milliseconds.

With DASD came a new piece of system software known as a DBMS or database management system. The purpose of the DBMS was to make it easy for the programmer to access data on DASD. In addition, the DBMS took care of such tasks as storing data on DASD, indexing data, and so forth. With DASD and DBMS came a technological solution to the problems of master files. And with DBMS came the notion of a "database." In looking at the mess that was created by master files and the masses of redundant data that aggregated on them, it is no wonder that database is defined as

database—a single source of data for all processing.

But the world did not end in 1970. By the mid-1970s, online transaction processing began to take place on databases. With a terminal and the appropriate software, the technician found that quicker access to data was possible—opening whole new vistas. With high-performance online transaction processing, the computer could be used for tasks not previously possible. The computer could now be used to drive reservations systems, bank teller systems, manufacturing control systems, and the like. Had the world remained in a magnetic tape file state, most of the systems that we take for granted today would not have been possible.

PC/4GL TECHNOLOGY

By the 1980s, more new technologies—such as PC and 4GL technology—began to surface. The end user began to assume a role previously unfathomed—directly controlling data and systems, outside the domain of the classical data processor. With PCs and 4GL technology came the notion that more could be done with data than servicing online high-performance transaction processing. MIS (management information systems)—as it was called in the early days—could also be done. Today known as DSS, MIS was processing that which was used to drive management decisions. Previously, data and technology were used exclusively to drive detailed operational decisions. There arose the notion of a paradigm—a single database that could serve both operational, high-performance transaction processing and DSS, analytical processing at the same time. Figure 1.1 shows the single database paradigm.

ENTER THE EXTRACT PROGRAM

Shortly after the advent of massive online high-performance transactions, there began to appear an innocuous program called an "extract" program, shown in Figure 1.2.

The extract program is the simplest of all programs. It rummages through a file or database, uses some criteria for selection, and, upon finding qualified data, transports the data over onto another file or database.

Soon the extract program became very popular. It permeated the information processing environment. There are (at least!) two reasons for its popularity.

- Because it can move data out of the way of high-performance online processing with an extract program, there is no conflict in terms of performance when the data needs to be analyzed en masse.
- When data is moved out of the operational, transaction processing domain with an extract program, there is a shift in control of the data. The end user ends up "owning" the data once he/she takes control of it.

For these (and probably a host of other) reasons, extract processing was soon found everywhere. By the 1990s, there were many, many extract programs, as depicted in Figure 1.3.

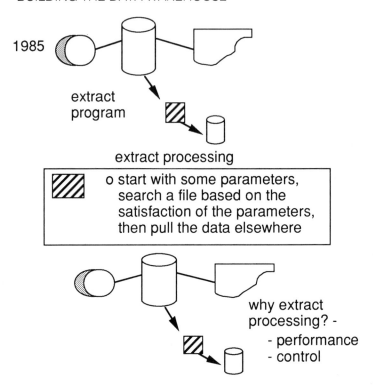

Figure 1.2.   Soon there was extract processing.

THE "SPIDER WEB"

Figure 1.3 shows that a "spider web" of extract processing began to form. First, there were extracts. Then there were extracts of extracts. Then extracts of extracts of extracts, and so forth. It was not unheard of for a large company to be doing as many as 45,000 extracts per day.

This pattern of extract processing across the organization became so commonplace that a name developed for it. Extract processing gone out of control produced what can be called the "naturally evolving architecture"—what occurs when an organization handles the whole process of hardware and software architecture with a laissez faire attitude. The larger and more mature the

naturally
evolving
architecture
(AKA the "spiderweb")

1990 -

Figure 1.3. Extract processing must have been a good
thing based on its widespread proliferation.

organization, the worse the problems of the naturally evolving
architecture become.

Taken collectively, the extract programs form a "spider web"—
just another name for the naturally evolving architecture.

Problems with the Naturally Evolving Architecture

What exactly are the problems associated with the naturally evolving architecture? There are many problems, principally

- credibility of data;
- productivity; and
- inability to transform data into information.

Lack of Credibility of Data

The first of these problems—the lack of credibility of data—is illustrated in Figure 1.4.

In Figure 1.4, two departments are delivering a report to management. One department states that activity is down 15 percent. The other department says that activity is up 10 percent. Not only are the two departments not in sync with each other, they are off by very large margins. In addition, trying to reconcile the departments is a

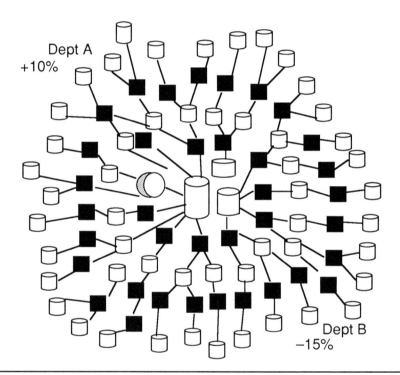

Figure 1.4.   Reasons for the predictability of the lack of credibility in the naturally evolving architecture:

- no time basis of data
- algorithmic differential
- levels of extraction
- external data
- no common source of data to begin with

very difficult thing to do. Unless very careful documentation has been done, reconciliation is—for all practical purposes—impossible.

When management receives the two reports, they do not know what to think. This is an example of the crisis in credibility in the naturally evolving architecture.

This crisis is widespread and predictable. Why?

Five reasons for the predictability of the crisis are

- no time basis of data;
- the algorithmic differential of data;
- the levels of extraction;
- the problem of external data; and
- no common source of data to begin with.

The lack of a time basis of data is illustrated in Figure 1.5.

Figure 1.5 shows that one department has extracted its data for analysis on a Sunday evening. The other department doing analysis has extracted data on a Wednesday afternoon. Is there any reason to believe that a sample of data taken on one day will be the same as a sample of data taken on another day? Of course not! Data are always changing within the corporation. Any correlation between analyzed sets of data that are taken at different points in time is only coincidental.

The second reason for the predictability of the crisis of credibility of data in the naturally evolving architecture is the algorithmic differential. For example, one department has chosen to analyze all old accounts. Another department has chosen to analyze all large accounts. Is there any necessary correlation between the characteristics of customers who have old accounts and customers who have large accounts? Probably not. So why should a very different result of analysis surprise anyone?

The third reason for predictability of crisis is one that merely magnifies the first two reasons. Every time a new extraction is done, the probabilities of a discrepancy arise because of the timing or the algorithmic differential. And it is not unusual for a corporation to have eight or nine levels of extraction being done from the time the data enter the corporation's system to the time analysis is prepared for management.

The fourth reason for lack of credibility is because of the problem

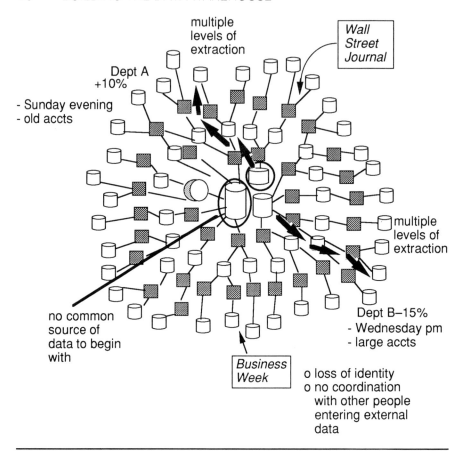

Figure 1.5.   The reasons for the predictability of the crisis in credibility in the naturally evolving architecture.

posed by external data. With today's technologies at the PC level, it is very easy to bring in data from outside sources. In the example shown in Figure 1.5, one analyst has brought data into the mainstream of analysis from the *Wall Street Journal*, and another analyst has brought data in from *Business Week*. The first thing the analyst does as he or she brings data in is to strip the external data of its identity. Instead of data originating from the *Wall Street Journal*, once the data is entered into the PC, it simply becomes plain data that could have come from any source.

Furthermore, the analyst who brings in data from the *Wall Street Journal* knows nothing about the data being entered from *BusinessWeek*, and vice versa. No wonder then that external data contributes to the lack of credibility of data in the naturally evolving architecture.

The last contributing factor to the lack of credibility is that often there is no common source of data to begin with. Analysis for department A originates from file XYZ. Analysis for department B originates from database ABC. And there is no synchronization or sharing of data whatsoever between file XYZ and database ABC.

Given these reasons then, it is no small wonder that there is a crisis of credibility brewing in every organization that allows its architecture of hardware, software, and data to evolve naturally into the spider's web.

The Problems with Productivity

But credibility of data is not the only major problem with the naturally evolving architecture. The productivity (or lack thereof) that is achieved in the naturally evolving architecture, when there is a need to look across the organization, is abysmal.

Consider an organization that has been in business for a while and has built up a large collection of data, as shown in the top of Figure 1.6.

Management desires to produce a corporate report, using the many files and collections of data that have accumulated over the years. The designer assigned the task decides there are three things that must be done to produce the corporate report.

- Locate the data for the report.
- Compile the data for the report.
- Get programmer/analyst resources to accomplish the above.

In order to locate the data, MANY files and layouts of data must be analyzed. Furthermore, there are complicating factors: One file has an element known as BALANCE; another file has an element with the same name. But the two elements are very different. In another case, one database has a file known as CURRBAL. In another collection of data, there is a file called INVLEVEL that happens to be the same as CURRBAL. This process of having to go

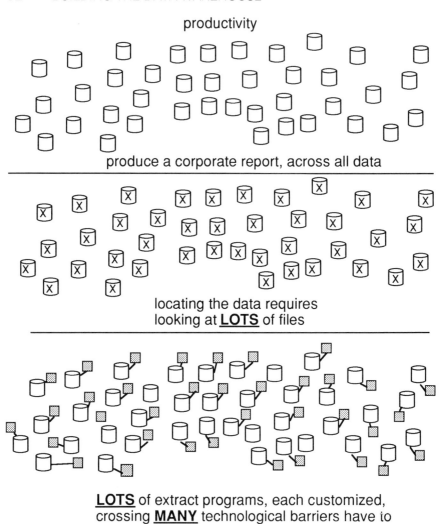

productivity

produce a corporate report, across all data

locating the data requires
looking at **LOTS** of files

LOTS of extract programs, each customized,
crossing **MANY** technological barriers have to
be crossed

Figure 1.6.   The naturally evolving architecture is not
conducive to productivity.

through every piece of data—not just by name but by definition and calculation—is a VERY tedious process. But if the corporate report is to be produced, this exercise MUST be done and done properly.

The next task is to compile the data, once located. Certainly the program that must be written to get data is a simple program. But it is complicated by the fact that

- there are lots of programs that have to be written;
- each program must be customized; and
- the programs cross every technology that the company has.

In short, even though the report-generation program must be written and appears to be simple to do, because of the above factors, retrieving the data for the corporate report is a very tedious activity.

In a recent corporation facing exactly the problems described, an analyst estimated a VERY long time to accomplish the tasks, as shown in Figure 1.7.

If the designer had asked for only two or three man-months of resources, then generating the report may not have required much management attention. But when an analyst requisitions many resources, management must put the request in with all the other requests for resources, and management must prioritize the requests. So, the analyst estimated a lengthy time to create the desired reports.

But creating the reports using a large amount of resources wouldn't be bad if there were a one-time penalty to be paid. In other words, if the first corporate report generated required a large amount of resources, and all succeeding reports could build on the first report, then it might be worthwhile to bite the bullet and pay the price for generating the first report. But such is not the case.

Unless future corporate reporting requirements are known in advance, and unless those requirements are factored into the building of the first corporate report, then there is every likelihood that every new corporate report is going to have to pay the same large overhead. In other words, it is highly unlikely that the first corporate report is going to do anything for future corporate reporting requirements.

Productivity, then, in the corporate environment is a very major issue in the face of the naturally evolving architecture.

productivity

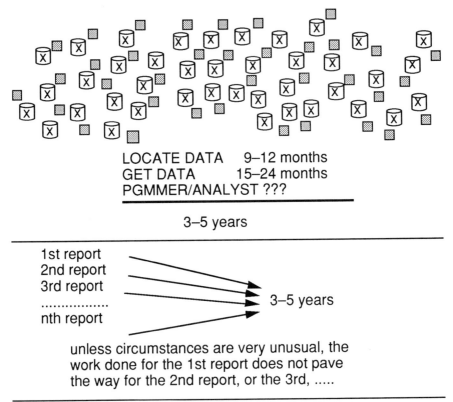

LOCATE DATA   9–12 months
GET DATA   15–24 months
PGMMER/ANALYST ???

3–5 years

1st report
2nd report
3rd report
....
nth report   3–5 years

unless circumstances are very unusual, the
work done for the 1st report does not pave
the way for the 2nd report, or the 3rd, ...

Figure 1.7. The requirements for succeeding reports are
not known at the time the first report is being
written.

From Data to Information

As if productivity and credibility were not problems enough, there
is another major fault of the naturally evolving architecture—the
inability to go from data to information. At first glance, the notion
of going from data to information seems to be an ethereal concept
with little substance. But such is not the case at all.

Consider the following request for information, typical in a
banking environment: "How has account activity been different
this year from each of the past five years for the bank?"

Figure 1.8 shows the request for information.

The first thing the DSS analyst encounters in trying to satisfy the request for information is that going to existing systems for the necessary data is about the worst place to go. The first thing the analyst will encounter there is lots of applications.

Trying to find out what data exists for an account is a difficult thing to do. There are savings applications. There are loans applications. There are DDA applications. There are trust applications.

going from data to information -

an example -

"How has account activity been different this year from each of the past five for the financial institute?"

loans

DDA

CD

passbook

first, you run into lots of applications

loans

DDA

CD

passbook

same element, different name

different element, same name

element exists only here

Figure 1.8. Next, you run into the lack of integration across applications.

going from data to information -
an example -
   "How has account activity been different this year from
   each of the past five for the financial institute?"

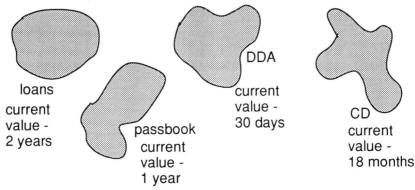

Figure 1.9.   Existing applications simply do not have the
historical data required to convert data into
information.

And trying to draw information from them on a common basis is
nigh impossible. The applications were never constructed with
integration in mind, and they are no easier for the DSS analyst to
decipher than they are for anyone else.

But integration is not the only difficulty the analyst meets in
trying to satisfy an informational request. A second major obstacle
is that there is not enough historical data stored in the applications
to meet the needs of the DSS request, as shown in Figure 1.9.

Figure 1.9 shows that the loans department has up to 2 years'
worth of data. Passbook processing has up to 1 year of data. DDA
applications have up to 60 days of data. And CD processing has up
to 18 months of data. The applications were built to service the
needs of current balance processing (naturally enough!). They were
never designed to hold the historical data needed for DSS analysis.
It is no wonder, then, that going to existing systems for DSS
analysis is a poor choice. But where else is there to go?

The systems found in the naturally evolving architecture are
simply inadequate for the task of supporting information needs.

A Change in Approaches

The status quo of the naturally evolving architecture—where most shops are at today—simply is not enough to meet the needs of tomorrow. What is needed is a change in architectures—where the architected data warehouse environment is found.

At the heart of an "architected" environment is the realization that there are fundamentally two kinds of data—primitive data and derived data. Figure 1.10 shows some of the major differences between primitive and derived data.

---

a change in approaches

PRIMITIVE DATA	DERIVED DATA
• detailed	• summarized, otherwise refined
• accurate, as of the moment of access	• represents values over time
• serves the clerical community	• serves the managerial community
• can be updated	• is not updated
• run repetitively	• run heuristically
• requirements for processing understood a priori	• requirements for processing not understood a priori
• compatible with the SDLC	• completely different life cycle
• performance sensitive	• performance relaxed
• accessed unit at a time	• accessed set at a time
• transaction driven	• analysis driven
• application oriented	• analysis oriented
• control of update is major concern in terms of ownership	• control of update - no issue
• high availability	• relaxed availability
• managed in its entirety	• managed by subsets
• nonredundancy	• redundancy is a fact of life
• static structure; variable contents	• flexible structure
• amount of data used in a process is small	• amount of data used in a process is large
• supports day-to-day operations	• supports managerial needs
• high probability of access	• low, modest probability of access

---

Figure 1.10.   The whole notion of data is changed in the architected environment.

Primitive data is that detailed data used to run the day-to-day operations of the company. Derived data is data that are summarized or otherwise calculated to meet the needs of the management of the company. Primitive data can be updated. Derived data cannot be updated. Primitive data is primarily current-value data. Derived data is often historical data. Primitive data is operated on by procedures that run in a repetitive fashion. Derived data is operated on by programs that run heuristically, on a nonrepetitive basis. Primitive data supports the clerical function. Derived data supports the managerial function.

Thus, there are then a host of differences between primitive and derived data. It is a wonder that the information processing community ever thought that both primitive and derived data would both fit in a single database.

THE ARCHITECTED ENVIRONMENT

The natural extension of the split in data caused by the difference between primitive and derived data is shown in Figure 1.11.

There are four levels in the architected environment—the operational, the atomic or the data warehouse, the departmental, and the individual. The operational level of data holds primitive data only and serves the high-performance transaction processing community. The data warehouse holds primitive data that is not updated. In addition, some derived data is found there. The departmental level of data contains derived data almost exclusively. And the individual level of data is where much heuristic analysis is done.

The immediate reaction to the architecture is that there is much redundant data in the architected environment. Such is not the case at all, although it is not obvious at first glance. Instead, the gross amounts of data redundancy are found in the spider's web.

Consider the simple example of data throughout the architecture, as shown in Figure 1.12.

Figure 1.12 shows that at the operational level there is a record for a customer, J Jones. The record at the operational level is the record that contains current value data. To learn the status of the customer right now, the record in the operational level is accessed. Of course, if the information for J Jones changes, the record in the operational level will be changed to reflect the new data that are correct.

levels of the architecture

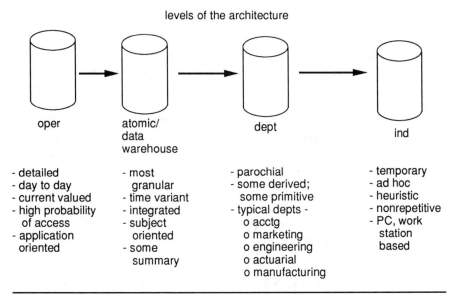

oper	atomic/ data warehouse	dept	ind

- detailed
- day to day
- current valued
- high probability
  of access
- application
  oriented
	- most
	  granular
	- time variant
	- integrated
	- subject
	  oriented
	- some
	  summary
		- parochial
		- some derived;
		  some primitive
		- typical depts -
		  o acctg
		  o marketing
		  o engineering
		  o actuarial
		  o manufacturing
			- temporary
			- ad hoc
			- heuristic
			- nonrepetitive
			- PC, work
			  station
			  based

Figure 1.11. Although it is not apparent at first glance, there is very little redundancy of data across the architected environment.

There are several records for J Jones that are found in the data warehouse environment. There records show the history of information about J Jones. To discover where J Jones lived last year, for example, the records in the data warehouse are searched. There is no overlap between the records in the operational environment and the data warehouse environment. If there is a change of address for J Jones, then a new record will be created in the data warehouse, reflecting the from and to dates that J Jones lived there. Note that the records in the data warehouse are not overlapping. Also note that there is some element of time associated with each record in the data warehouse.

The departmental environment contains information useful to the different parochial departments of a company. There is a marketing departmental database, an accounting departmental database, an actuarial departmental database, and so forth. The source of ALL departmental data is the data warehouse.

Typical of data at the departmental level is a monthly customer file. In the file is a list of all customers by category. Into this

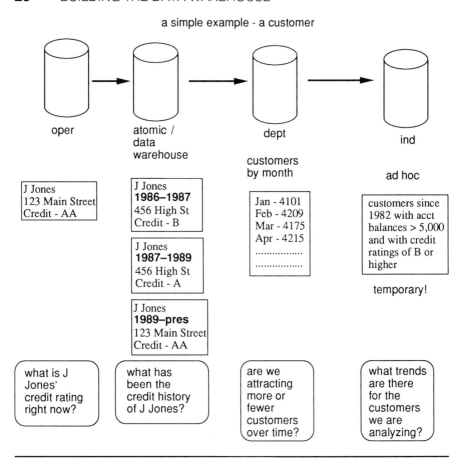

Figure 1.12.   The kinds of queries that the different levels of data can be used for.

summary goes J Jones each month. It is a stretch to consider the tallying of information as a form of redundancy.

The final level of data is the individual level of data. Individual data are temporary. At the individual level much heuristic analysis is done. As a rule, the individual levels of data are thought of as being supported by the PC. EIS processing typically runs on the individual levels.

Integration

One important aspect of the architected environment that is not shown in Figure 1.12 is the integration of data that occur across the architecture. As data pass from the operational environment to the data warehouse environment, they are integrated, as shown in Figure 1.13.

Figure 1.13.   As data is transformed from the operational environment to the data warehouse environment, it is integrated as well.

There is no point in bringing data over from the operational environment into the data warehouse environment WITHOUT integrating it. If the data arrives at the data warehouse in an unintegrated state, it cannot be used to support a corporate view of data. And a corporate view of data is precisely the essence of the architected environment.

THE DEVELOPMENT LIFE CYCLE

While operational data are usually unintegrated and, of necessity, data warehouse data must be integrated, there are other major differences between the operational level of data and processing and the data warehouse level of data and processing. Another profound difference between the operational level and the data warehouse level is that of the underlying development life cycle, as shown in Figure 1.14.

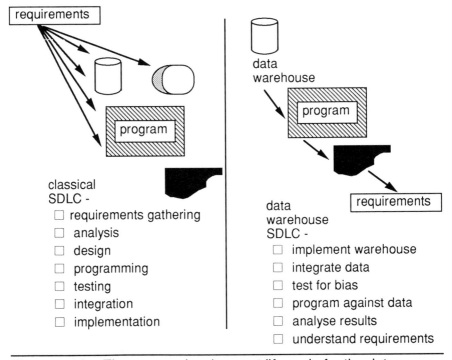

Figure 1.14. The system development life cycle for the data warehouse environment is almost perfectly the opposite of the classical SDLC.

Figure 1.14 shows that the operational environment is supported by the classical systems development life cycle (the SDLC). The data warehouse operates under a very different life cycle, sometimes called the CLDS (the reverse of the SDLC). The classical SDLC is requirements driven. In order to build systems, you must first understand the requirements. Then you go into stages of design and development. The CLDS is almost the reverse. The CLDS starts with data. Once data are in hand, it is integrated then tested to see what bias there is to the data, if any. Programs are then written against the data. The results of the programs are analyzed, and finally, the requirements of the system are understood.

The CLDS is a classic data-driven development life cycle, while the SDLC is a classic requirements development life cycle. Trying to apply tools and techniques of development that are appropriate elsewhere only results in waste and confusion. For example, the CASE world is dominated by requirements-driven analysis. Trying to apply CASE tools and techniques to the world of data warehouse is not advisable, and vice versa.

PATTERNS OF HARDWARE UTILIZATION

Yet another major difference between the operational and the data warehouse environments is the patterns of hardware utilization that occur in each environment. Figure 1.15 shows the difference.

The left-hand side of the figure shows the classic pattern of hardware utilization for operational processing. There are peaks and valleys in operational processing, but ultimately, there is a relatively static pattern of utilization.

There is an essentially different pattern of hardware utilization in the data warehouse environment (shown on the right-hand side of the figure)—a binary pattern of utilization. Either the hardware is being utilized fully or not at all. Calculating a mean percentage of utilization for the data warehouse environment is not a meaningful activity.

This fundamental difference is one more reason why trying to mix the two environments on the same machine at the same time does not work. You can either optimize your machine for operational processing, or you can optimize your machine for data ware-

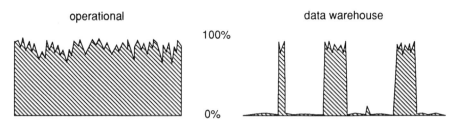

Figure 1.15.   The different patterns of hardware utilization in
the different environments.

house processing, but you cannot do both at the same time on the
same piece of equipment.

SUMMARY

This chapter has discussed the architecture into which the data
warehouse environment fits. The architecture has evolved through
the history of the different stages of information processing. There
are four levels of data and processing in the architecture—the
operational level, the data warehouse level, the departmental level,
and the individual level.

2

The Data Warehouse Environment

At the heart of the architected environment is the data warehouse. The data warehouse is the foundation of DSS processing. Because there is a single integrated source of data in the data warehouse, and because the data are accessible, the job of the DSS analyst in the data warehouse environment is immeasurably easier than in the classical environment.

This chapter will describe some of the more important aspects of the data warehouse.

SUBJECT ORIENTED

The data warehouse is subject oriented, oriented to the major subject areas of the corporation that have been defined in the data model. Typical subject areas are

- customer
- product
- transaction or activity
- policy
- claim
- account, etc.

The major subject area ends up being physically implemented as a series of related tables in the data warehouse. For example, a customer implementation might look like that shown in Figure 2.1.

There are five related tables in Figure 2.1, each of which has been designed to implement a part of a major subject area—customer.

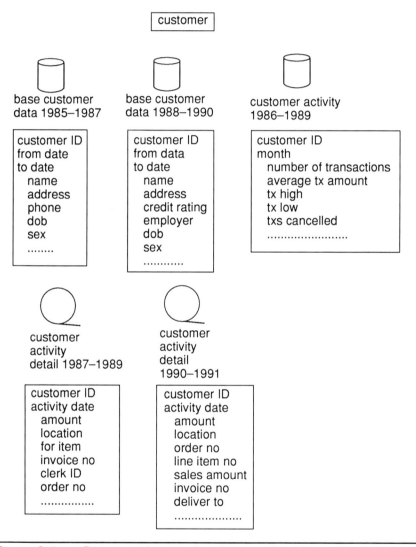

Figure 2.1. Data warehouse data is organized by major subject area—in this case by customer.

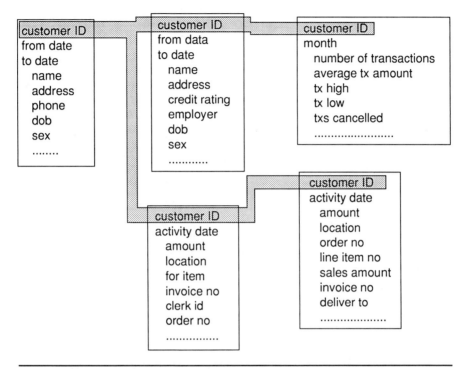

Figure 2.2.   The collections of data that belong to the same subject area are tied together by a common key.

There is a base table for customer information for customer data as defined from 1985 to 1987. There is another for the definition of customer data between 1988 and 1990. There is a cumulative customer activity table for customer activities between 1986 and 1989. Each month a summary record is written for each customer record based upon the activity the customer had for the month.

There are detailed activity files by customer for 1987 through 1989 and another one for 1990 through 1991. The definition of the data in the files is different, based on the year.

All of the tables for one customer are related by a common key, as shown in Figure 2.2.

Figure 2.2 shows that the key—customer ID—connects all of the data found in the customer subject area. Another interesting aspect of the customer subject area is that it may reside on different media, as shown in Figure 2.3.

Figure 2.3.   The subject area may contain data on different media in the data warehouse.

Figure 2.3 shows that some of the data reside on DASD and some reside on magnetic tape. One implication of data residing on different media is that there may be more than one DBMS managing the data in a warehouse, or that some data may not be managed by a DBMS at all. Just because data resides on magnetic tape does not mean it is not a part of the data warehouse.

Data that has a high probability of access and a low volume of storage resides on a medium that is fast and relatively expensive. Data that has a low probability of access and that is bulky resides on a medium that is cheaper and that is slow to access.

As a rule DASD and magnetic tape are the two most popular media on which to store data in a data warehouse. But they are not the only media. Two other media that should not be overlooked are fiche and optical disk. Fiche is good for storing detailed records that never have to be reproduced in an electronic medium again. Legal records are often stored on fiche for an indefinite period of time. Optical disk storage is especially good for data warehouse storage because it is cheap, relatively fast, and able to hold a mass of data. Another reason why optical disk is useful is because data warehouse data, once written, is seldom, if ever, updated. This last characteristic makes optical disk storage a very desirable choice for data warehouses.

Another interesting aspect of the files (shown in Figure 2.3) is that there is both a level of summary and a level of detail for the same data. Activity by month is summarized. The detail that supports activity by month is stored at the magnetic tape level of data. This is a form of a "shift in granularity" which will be discussed at length later.

When data are organized around the subject—the customer— each key has an element of time as part of the key, as shown in Figure 2.4.

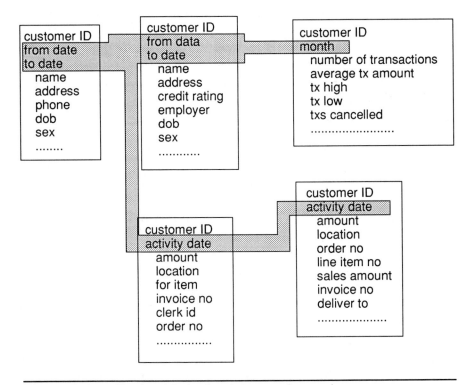

Figure 2.4.   Each table in the data warehouse has an element of time as a part of the key structure, usually the lower part.

Some tables are organized on a "from date to date" basis. This is called a continuous organization of data. Other tables are organized on a cumulative monthly basis, and others on an individual date of record or activity basis. But all records have some form of data attached to the key, usually the lower part of the key.

DAY 1—DAY N PHENOMENA

Data warehouses are not built all at once. Instead, data warehouses are designed and populated a step at a time, and as such are evolutionary, not revolutionary. The costs of building a data warehouse all at once, the resources required, the disruption to the environment, all dictate that the data warehouse be built in an orderly, step at a time fashion.

The typical process of building a data warehouse is illustrated by Figure 2.5.

Figure 2.5 shows that on day one there is a polyglot of systems doing essentially operational processing. On day two, the first few tables of the first subject area of the data warehouse are populated. At this point a certain amount of curiosity is raised, and the users start to discover data warehouses.

On day three, more of the data warehouse is populated. And with the population of more data come more users. Once users find there is an integrated source of data that is easy to get to and has a historical basis that is made for looking at data over the spectrum of time, there is more than curiosity. At about this time, the serious DSS analyst becomes attracted to the data warehouse.

On day four, even more of the warehouse becomes populated. Some of the data that had resided in the operational environment become properly placed in the data warehouse. And the data warehouse is now "discovered" as a source for doing analytical processing. All sorts of DSS applications spring up. Indeed, there start to appear so many users and so many requests for processing, coupled with a rather large volume of data that now reside in the warehouse, that some users begin to be put off by the work and effort required to get to the data warehouse. The competition to get at the warehouse becomes an obstacle to its usage.

On day five, departmental databases start to blossom. Depart-

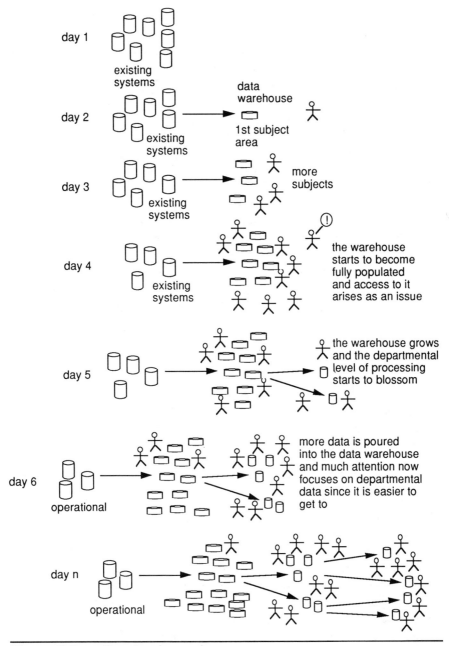

Figure 2.5.   Day 1—day n phenomenon.

ments find that it is cheaper and easier to get their processing done by bringing data from the data warehouse into their own departmental processing environment. As data go to the departmental level, a few DSS analysts are attracted.

On day six, the landrush to departmental systems takes place. It is cheaper, faster, and easier to get departmental data than it is to get data from the data warehouse. Soon end users are weaned from the data warehouse to departmental processing.

On day n, the architecture is fully developed. All that is left of the original set of production systems is operational processing. The warehouse is full of data. There are a few direct users of the data warehouse. There are a lot of departmental databases. Most of the DSS analytical processing occurs at the departmental level because it is easier and cheaper to get the data needed for processing there.

Of course, evolution from day one to day n takes a long time. Several years is the norm. And all during the process of moving from day one to day n the DSS environment is up and functional.

GRANULARITY

The single most important aspect of design of a data warehouse is the issue of granularity. Granularity refers to the level of detail held in the units of data in the data warehouse. The more detail there is, the lower the level of granularity. The less detail there is, the higher the level of granularity.

Granularity of data has always been a design issue. In the early operational systems that were built, granularity was taken for granted. When detailed data are being updated, it is almost a given that data be stored at the lowest level of granularity. But in the data warehouse environment, granularity is NOT assumed.

Figure 2.6 illustrates the issues of granularity.

The reason why granularity is THE major design issue in the data warehouse environment is that it profoundly affects the volume of data that reside in the data warehouse and at the same time affects the type of query that can be answered. The volume of data in a warehouse must be traded off in order to satisfy a query.

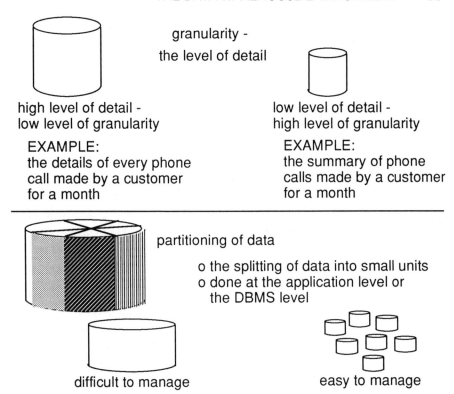

granularity -
the level of detail

high level of detail -
low level of granularity

EXAMPLE:
the details of every phone
call made by a customer
for a month

low level of detail -
high level of granularity

EXAMPLE:
the summary of phone
calls made by a customer
for a month

partitioning of data

o the splitting of data into small units
o done at the application level or
the DBMS level

difficult to manage   easy to manage

Figure 2.6.   Major design issues of the data warehouse.

- granularity
- partitioning
- proper design

PARTITIONING

The second major design issue of data in the warehouse is that of
partitioning. Partitioning of data refers to the breakup of data into
separate physical units that can be handled independently. In the
data warehouse, the issues surrounding partitioning do not focus
on whether partitioning should be done but how it should be done.

It is often said that if both granularity and partitioning are done
properly, then almost all other aspects of the data warehouse
design and implementation come easily. But if granularity is not

handled properly and if partitioning is not designed and implemented carefully, then no other aspects of design really matter.

Of course, there are other design aspects of the data warehouse that will be discussed in later chapters.

An Example of Granularity

Figure 2.7 shows an example of the issues of granularity.

On the left-hand side of Figure 2.7 there is a low level of granularity. Each activity—in this case, a phone call—is recorded in detail. The layout of the data is shown. At the end of the month, each customer has on the average 200 records (one for each recorded phone call throughout the month) that require about 40,000 bytes collectively.

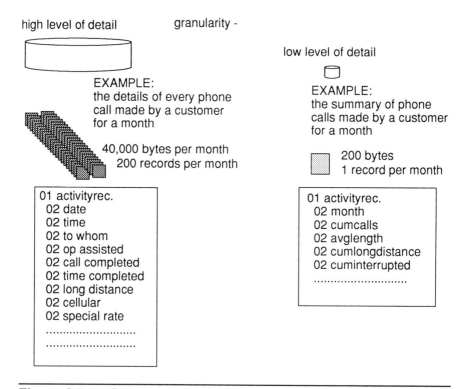

Figure 2.7.   Determining the level of granularity is the most important design issue in the data warehouse environment.

On the right-hand side of the figure is a higher level of granularity. The data represent the summary information for a customer for a month. There is one record for each customer for a month, and that record requires about 200 bytes. The layout of the record is shown.

It is obvious that if space is a problem in a data warehouse, (and volume of data is ALWAYS the first and major issue in the data warehouse) a high level of granularity is a much more efficient way of representing data than a representation using a low level of granularity.

Not only are many fewer bytes of data required with a higher level of granularity, but fewer index entries are needed. But the volume of data and the issue of raw space are not the only relevant issues. The amount of processing power that needs to be used in the face of a large volume of data in order to access the data is a factor as well.

There is then a very good case for the compaction of data in a data warehouse. When data is compacted there are nontrivial savings in the

- amount of DASD used,
- the number of index entries required and
- the processor resources required to manipulate data.

But there is another aspect to the compaction of data that occurs when the level of granularity is raised. Figure 2.8 shows the tradeoff that is made.

In Figure 2.8 it is seen that as the level of granularity of data rises, there is a corresponding loss in the capability of using the data to answer queries. Put another way, with a very low level of granularity, you can answer practically any query. But with a high level of granularity, the number of questions that the data can handle is limited.

In Figure 2.8 the following query is made:

"Did Jeff Caplan call his girlfriend in Peoria last week?"

With a low level of granularity, the query can be answered. It may take a lot of resources to thumb through a lot of records, but at the end of the day, whether or not Jeff called his girlfriend in Peoria last week can be determined.

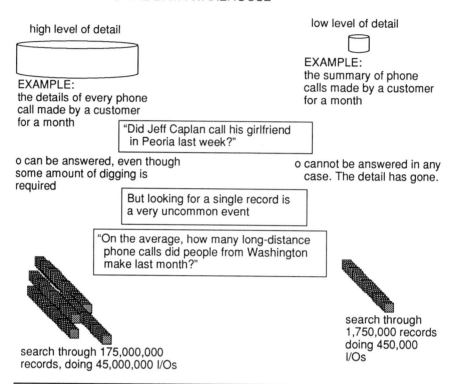

high level of detail

EXAMPLE:
the details of every phone
call made by a customer
for a month

low level of detail

EXAMPLE:
the summary of phone
calls made by a customer
for a month

"Did Jeff Caplan call his girlfriend
in Peoria last week?"

o can be answered, even though
some amount of digging is
required

o cannot be answered in any
case. The detail has gone.

But looking for a single record is
a very uncommon event

"On the average, how many long-distance
phone calls did people from Washington
make last month?"

search through
1,750,000 records
doing 450,000
I/Os

search through 175,000,000
records, doing 45,000,000 I/Os

Figure 2.8.   The level of granularity has a profound effect both
on what questions can be answered and on what
resources are required to answer a question.

But with a high level of detail, there is no way to definitively answer the question. If all that is kept about Jeff Caplan in the data warehouse is the total number of calls that he made, no determination can be made whether one of those calls went to Peoria.

But when doing DSS processing, as is common in the data warehouse environment, it is rare that only a single event is examined. It is much more common that a collective view of data be viewed. This means looking at a large number of records.

For example, suppose the following collective query is made:

"On the average, how many long-distance phone calls did people from Washington make last month?"

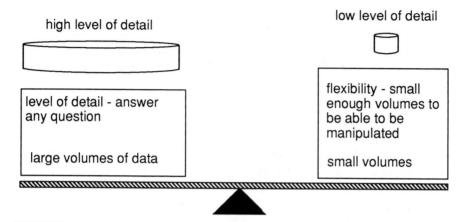

high level of detail

low level of detail

level of detail - answer any question	flexibility - small enough volumes to be able to be manipulated
large volumes of data	small volumes

Figure 2.9. The tradeoffs with granularity are so marked and so stark that for most organizations the best solution is some form of multiple levels of granularity.

This type of query is very normal in a DSS environment. Of course, it can be answered by both the high level and the low level of granularity. But in answering it, there is a tremendous difference in the resources used. To answer this query in the low level of granularity case requires going through every record. Many, many resources are required to answer this question.

But using the high level of granularity data, the data are much more compact and able to provide an answer. It is MUCH MORE efficient to use the high level of granularity data if it contains sufficient detail to be used.

The tradeoff, then, in managing the issue of granularity of data is shown in Figure 2.9.

This tradeoff must be considered VERY carefully at the outset in the design and the construction of the data warehouse.

Dual Levels of Granularity

Most of the time, there is a great need for efficiency in storing data and its access AND the ability to analyze data in great detail. (In other words, the organization wants to have its cake and eat it, too!) When an organization has lots of data in the warehouse, it makes eminent sense to consider two (or more!) levels of granularity in the data warehouse. In fact, the need for more than one level of granularity is such that the dual level of granularity design option should be the default for almost every shop. Figure 2.10 shows two levels of granularity.

Called a "dual" level of granularity, the design shown in Figure 2.10—a phone company—fits the needs of most shops. At the operational level is a tremendous amount of detail. Most of this detail is needed for the billing systems. Up to 30 days of detail is stored in the operational level.

The data warehouse contains two types of data—lightly summarized data and "true archival" data. The data in the data warehouse

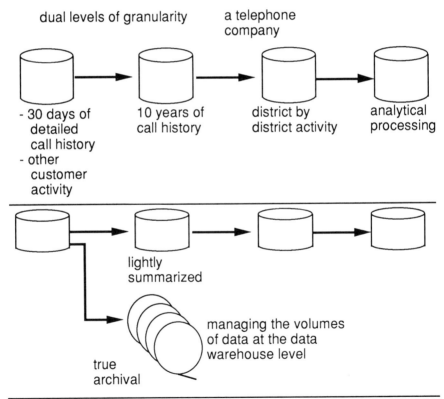

Figure 2.10. The volume of data is such that most organizations need to have two levels of granularity in the data warehouse.

can go back 10 years. The data that emanates from the data warehouse is "district" data that flows to the different districts the telephone company has. Each district then analyzes its data independently from other districts. At the individual level much heuristic analytical processing occurs.

It may not be immediately obvious what is meant by a light level of summarization. Figure 2.11 shows such a summarization.

As data are passed from the operational, 30-day store of data, it is summarized, by customer, into fields that are likely to be used for DSS analysis. The record for J Jones shows the number of calls made per month, the average length of each call, the number of

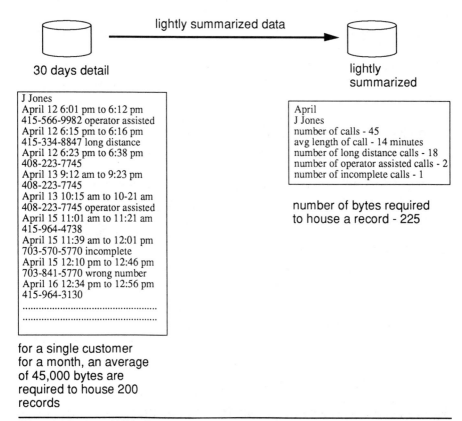

lightly summarized data

30 days detail

lightly summarized

J Jones
April 12 6:01 pm to 6:12 pm
415-566-9982 operator assisted
April 12 6:15 pm to 6:16 pm
415-334-8847 long distance
April 12 6:23 pm to 6:38 pm
408-223-7745
April 13 9:12 am to 9:23 pm
408-223-7745
April 13 10:15 am to 10-21 am
408-223-7745 operator assisted
April 15 11:01 am to 11:21 am
415-964-4738
April 15 11:39 am to 12:01 pm
703-570-5770 incomplete
April 15 12:10 pm to 12:46 pm
703-841-5770 wrong number
April 16 12:34 pm to 12:56 pm
415-964-3130
....
....

April
J Jones
number of calls - 45
avg length of call - 14 minutes
number of long distance calls - 18
number of operator assisted calls - 2
number of incomplete calls - 1

number of bytes required
to house a record - 225

for a single customer
for a month, an average
of 45,000 bytes are
required to house 200
records

Figure 2.11. With light summarization of data, large quantities of data can be represented very compactly.

long-distance calls made, the number of operator-assisted calls, and so forth.

There is significantly less volume of data in the lightly summarized database than there is in the detailed database. Of course, there is a limit to the level of detail that can be accessed in the lightly summarized database.

The second tier of data in the data warehouse—the lowest level of granularity—is stored in the "true archival" level of data, as shown in Figure 2.12.

At the true archival level of data, ALL the detail coming from the operational environment is stored. There is truly a multitude of data at this level. For that reason, it makes sense to store the data on a medium such as magnetic tape because the volume of data is so large.

By creating two levels of granularity in the data warehouse, the DSS architect has killed two birds with one stone—most DSS processing goes against the lightly summarized data where the data is compact and efficiently accessed. But on those occasions where some great level of detail must be delved into—5 percent of the time or less—there is the true archival level of data. It is expensive, cumbersome, and complex to access data at the true archival level of granularity. But if there is a necessity to go to that level of detail, it is there.

Over time, should there develop a pattern of searching the true archival level of data, the designer may want to create some new fields of data at the lightly summarized level of data in order to elevate the processing from the true archival to the lightly summarized level.

Because of the costs, efficiencies, ease of access, and ability to answer any query that can be answered, the dual level of data is the best architectural choice for the data warehouse for most shops. Only when a shop has a relatively small amount of data in the data warehouse environment should a single level of data be attempted.

LIVING SAMPLE DATA

An interesting offshoot of a shift in the granularity of data is the "living sample" database. This is merely a subset of either true archival data or lightly summarized data. The term "living sample" dual levels of granularity

April
J Jones
number of calls - 45
avg length of call - 14 minutes
number of long distance calls - 18
number of operator assisted calls - 2
number of incomplete calls - 1

lightly
summarized

95% or more of DSS
processing done here

5% or less of DSS
processing done here

J Jones
April 12 6:01 pm to 6:12 pm
415-566-9982 operator assisted
April 12 6:15 pm to 6:16 pm
415-334-8847 long distance
April 12 6:23 pm to 6:38 pm
408-223-7745
April 13 9:12 am to 9:23 pm
408-223-7745
April 13 10:15 am to 10-21 am
408-223-7745 operator assisted
April 15 11:01 am to 11:21 am
415-964-4738
April 15 11:39 am to 12:01 pm
703-570-5770 incomplete
April 15 12:10 pm to 12:46 pm
703-841-5770 wrong number
April 16 12:34 pm to 12:56 pm
415-964-3130
....
....

true
archival

o time consuming
o complex
o $$$$

Figure 2.12.   Dual levels of granularity allow you to

- efficiently process the vast majority of requests, and
- answer any question that can be answered.

In short, it is the best of all worlds and should be the default design choice.

stems from the fact that the living sample database is a subset—a sample—of a larger database, and that the living sample database needs to be periodically refreshed. Figure 2.13 shows a living sample database.

In some circumstances (for example, statistical analysis of a population), a living sample database can be very useful. But there are some severe restrictions with a living sample database, and the designer should not build such a database as part of the data warehouse unless he/she is aware of the limitations.

A living sample database is *not* a general purpose database. If you wanted to find out whether J Jones is a customer, you would not look into a living sample database for that information. It is absolutely possible for J Jones to be a customer but not be on record. Living

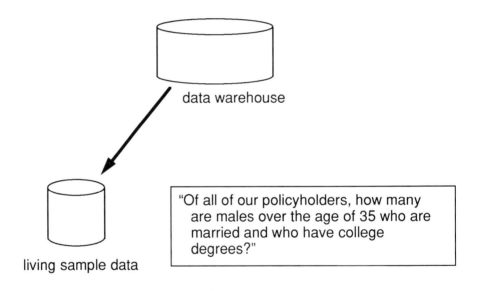

data warehouse

"Of all of our policyholders, how many are males over the age of 35 who are married and who have college degrees?"

living sample data

o a fraction of data in the warehouse
o used for very efficient formulation
  of a query
o <u>CANNOT BE USED FOR GENERAL PURPOSE
  ANALYSIS - CAN ONLY BE USED FOR
  STATISTICAL ANALYSIS</u>

Figure 2.13. Living sample data—another form of changing the granularity of data.

sample databases are good for statistical analysis and looking at trends. Where data must be looked at collectively, living sample databases can offer some very promising results, but they are not good at all for dealing with individual records of data.

Consider how a living sample database is typically loaded. A program rummages through a large database selecting every one hundredth or every one thousandth record. The record is then shipped to the living sample. The resulting living sample database, then, is 1/100 or 1/1000 the size of the original database.

The selection of records of the living sample is usually random. On occasion, a "judgment sample" is taken—one where a record must meet certain criteria in order to be selected. The problem with judgment samples is that they almost always introduce bias into the living sample data. The problem with a random selection of data is that it may not produce statistical significance. In any case, data are selected for the living sample. Because any given record is not found in the living sample database means nothing.

The greatest asset of a living sample database is that it is very efficient to access. Given that it is a fraction of the size of the larger database from which it was derived, it is correspondingly much more efficient to access and analyze.

Put another way, suppose an analyst takes 24 hours to scan and analyze a large database. It may take as little as 10 minutes to scan and analyze a living sample database. In doing heuristic analysis, the turnaround time is crucial to the analysis that can be done. In heuristic analysis, the analyst runs a program, studies the results, reformulates the program, and runs it again. If it takes 24 hours to execute the program, the process of analysis and reformulation is greatly impaired (not to mention the resources required to do the reformulation).

But with a living sample database that is small enough to be scanned in 10 minutes, the analyst can go through the iterative process very quickly. In short, the productivity of the DSS analyst depends on the speed of turning around the analysis being done.

There is the argument that doing statistical analysis yields incorrect answers. Consider the case where an analyst runs against a large file using 25,000,000 records to determine that 56.7% of the drivers on the road are men. Using a living sample database, the analyst uses 25,000 records to determine that 55.9% of the drivers on the road are men. One analysis has required vastly more resources than the other. Yet, the difference between the answers that have been calculated is very, very small. Undoubtedly, the analysis against the large database was more accurate, but the cost of that accuracy is exorbitant, especially in the face of heuristic processing where iterations of processing are the norm.

If very high degrees of accuracy are desired, a useful technique is to formulate the request and go through the iterative processing on the living sample database. In doing so, the DSS analyst quickly formulates the request. Then, when the request is understood, it is run one final time against the large database.

Living sample data is just one more form of changing the level of granularity in the data warehouse to accommodate DSS processing.

PARTITIONING OF DATA

There are two major issues in the data warehouse environment: the granularity of data and the partitioning of data. In the data warehouse environment, the question is not *whether* data will be partitioned but *how* data will be partitioned. Figure 2.14 illustrates partitioning.

The whole purpose of partitioning of data is to break data up into small physical units. Why is this so important? Small physical units afford the operations staff and the designer much more flexibility in the management of data than do large physical units.

When data resides in large physical units, it cannot be

- restructured easily,
- indexed freely,
- sequentially scanned, if needed,
- reorganized easily,
- recovered easily,
- monitored easily, and so forth.

In short, one of the essences of the data warehouse is the flexible access of data. Having a big mass of data defeats much of the purpose of the data warehouse. Therefore, ALL DATA WAREHOUSE DATA WILL BE PARTITIONED.

partitioning of data

small units of data can be
  o restructured
  o indexed
  o sequentially scanned, if needed
  o reorganized
  o recovered
  o monitored

1989

1988

independently managed units of data
can have different definitions

1990

1991

1987

processing
complex A

processing
complex B

Figure 2.14.   Independently managed partitions of data can
be sent to different processing complexes with
no other system considerations.

What exactly does it mean to partition data? Data is partitioned
when data of a like structure is divided into more than one physical
unit of data. In addition, any given unit of data fits on one and only
one partition.

There are many criteria by which data can be divided, for
example:

- by date,
- by line of business,
- by geography,
- by organizational unit, or
- by all of the above.

The choices for partitioning data are strictly up to the developer. However, in the data warehouse environment it is almost mandatory that one of the criteria for partitioning be by date.

As an example of how a life insurance company may choose to partition their data, consider the following physical units of data:

- 1988 health claims
- 1989 health claims
- 1990 health claims
- 1987 life claims
- 1988 life claims
- 1989 life claims
- 1990 life claims
- 1988 casualty claims
- 1989 casualty claims
- 1990 casualty claims

The insurance company has used the criteria of date—that is, year—and type of claim to partition the data.

One of the major issues facing the data warehouse developer is whether to do partitioning at the system level or at the application level. Partitioning at the system level is a function of the DBMS and the operating system to some extent. Partitioning at the application level is done by application code and is solely and strictly controlled by the developer and the programmer. The DBMS and the system know of no relation between one partition and the other when data is partitioned at the application level.

As a rule, it makes sense to partition data warehouse data at the application level. There are some important reasons for this. The most important is that at the application level there can be a different definition of data for each year. There can be 1988's definition of data and there can be 1989's definition of data, which may or may not bear a resemblance to 1988's definition. The nature of data in a warehouse is the collection of data over a long period of time.

When the partitioning is done at the system level, the DBMS inevitably wants a single definition of data. Given that the data warehouse holds data for a long period of time—up to 10 years—and given that the definition regularly changes, it does not make sense to allow the DBMS or the operating system to dictate that there should be a single definition of data.

Another important feature of allowing the partitioning of data to be managed at the application level is that it can be moved from one processing complex to another with impunity. When the workload and volume of data become a real burden in the data warehouse environment, this feature may be a real advantage.

The acid test for partitioning of data is to ask the question "Can an index be added to a partition with no discernible interruption to other operations?" If an index can be added at will, then the partition is fine enough. If an index cannot be added easily, then the partition needs to be broken down more finely.

STRUCTURING DATA IN THE DATA WAREHOUSE

So far, there has been much discussion of the data warehouse without going into what the data structures found in the data warehouse really look like. There are many kinds of structures found in the data warehouse. We will look at some of the more common ones now.

Perhaps the simplest and most common data structure found in the data warehouse is the simple cumulative structure, shown in Figure 2.15.

Figure 2.15 shows that the daily transactions are transported from the operational environment. After being transported, they are summarized into data warehouse records. The summarization may be by customer, account, or whatever subject area the data warehouse is organized into. The transactions are summarized by day. In other words, all daily activity for a customer for an account are totalled and passed into the data warehouse on a day-by-day basis.

Figure 2.16 shows a variation of the simple daily cumulation called the storage of rolling summary data.

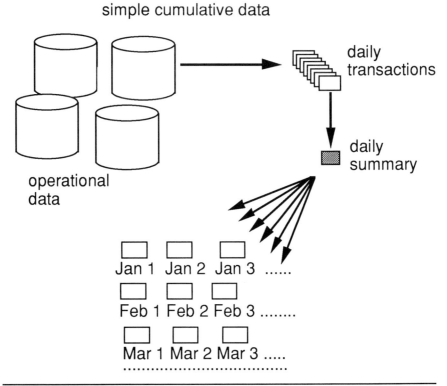

simple cumulative data

daily transactions

daily summary

operational data

Jan 1 Jan 2 Jan 3 ......

Feb 1 Feb 2 Feb 3 ....

Mar 1 Mar 2 Mar 3 .....

Figure 2.15.   The simplest form of data in the data warehouse is that of data that has been accumulated on a record-by-record basis—called simple cumulative data.

The data passes from the operational environment to the data warehouse environment as it did previously. Only in rolling summary data, the data is entered into a very different structure. For the first seven days of the week, activity is summarized into seven daily slots. On the eighth day, the seven daily slots are added together and placed into the first weekly slot. Then the daily totals are added into the first daily slot.

At the end of the month, the weekly slots are added together and placed in the first monthly slot. Then the weekly slots are reset to zero. At the end of the year, the monthly slots are added together,

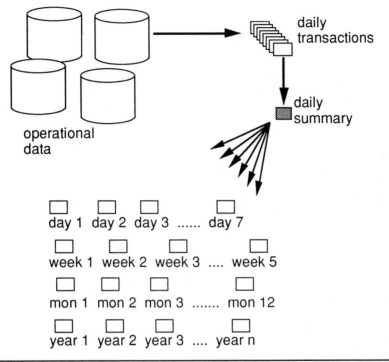

Figure 2.16.　A variation of the cumulative file is the rolling summary file.

and the first yearly slot is loaded. Then the monthly slots are reset to zero.

A rolling summary data structure handles data with many fewer units of data than does a simple cumulative structuring of data. A comparison of the advantages and the disadvantages of rolling summary versus simple cumulative structuring of data is shown in Figure 2.17.

Another possibility for the structuring of data warehouse data is the simple direct file, shown in Figure 2.18.

Figure 2.18 shows that data is merely pulled from the operational environment to the data warehouse environment. There is no accumulation that occurs. In addition, the simple direct file is not done on a daily basis. It is instead done over a longer period of time, such as a week, or a month. As such, the simple direct file

ROLLING SUMMARY DATA

☐ ☐ ☐   ☐
day 1 day 2 day 3 ...... day 7

☐   ☐   ☐   ☐   o very compact
week 1 week 2 week 3 .... week 5   o some loss of detail
                                    o the older data gets, the less
☐   ☐   ☐   ☐   detail is kept
mon 1 mon 2 mon 3 .... mon 12

☐   ☐   ☐   ☐
year 1 year 2 year 3 .... year n

SIMPLE CUMULATIVE DATA

☐ ☐ ☐   o much storage required
Jan 1 Jan 2 Jan 3 ......   o no loss of detail
                           o much processing to do
☐ ☐ ☐   anything with data
Feb 1 Feb 2 Feb 3 ....

☐ ☐ ☐
Mar 1 Mar 2 Mar 3 .....
....

Figure 2.17. Comparing simple cumulative data with rolling summary data.

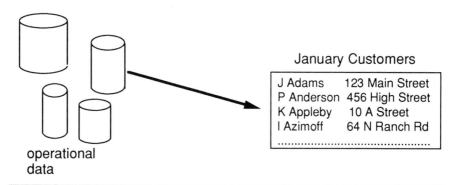

January Customers

J Adams	123 Main Street
P Anderson	456 High Street
K Appleby	10 A Street
I Azimoff	64 N Ranch Rd

operational data

Figure 2.18. A simple direct file, another data warehouse structure.

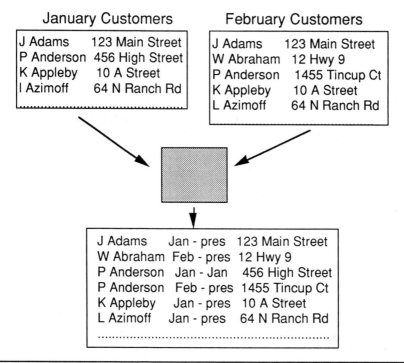

Figure 2.19. Creating a continuous file from direct files.

represents a snapshot of operational data taken as of some one instant in time.

From two or more simple direct files can be created a continuous file, as shown in Figure 2.19.

Figure 2.19 shows that two snapshots—one from January and one from February—are merged together to create a continuous file of data. The data in the continuous file represents the data continuously from the first month to the last.

Of course, a continuous file can be created by appending a snapshot of data onto a previous version of the continuous file, as shown in Figure 2.10.

There are MANY more structurings of data within the data warehouse. Shown here are

- simple cumulative,
- rolling summary,
- simple direct, and
- continuous.

These are only the most common.

At the key level, data warehouse keys are inevitably compounded keys. There are two compelling reasons for this.

- Date—year, year/month, year/month/day, etc., is almost always a part of the key.
- Because data warehouse data is partitioned, the different components of the partitioning show up as part of the key.

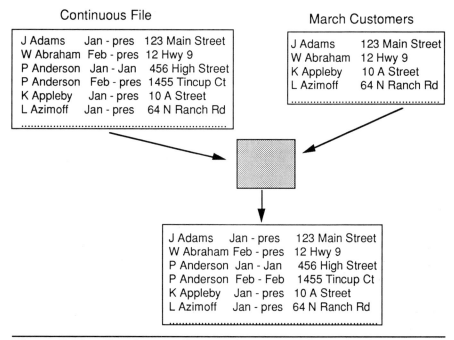

Figure 2.20. Continuous files can be created from simple direct files, or continuous files may have simple direct files appended onto them.

DATA WAREHOUSE—AN EXPLANATION

The data warehouse is relevant to many people—managers, DSS analysts, developers, planners, and so forth. In most organizations, data warehouse is new. Accordingly, there needs to be an "official" organizational explanation and description of the data warehouse.

It is probably deadly to call the warehouse explanation a "standards manual." Standards manuals have a dreary connotation and are famous for being ignored and gathering dust. Yet, some form of internal publication is a very worthwhile endeavor.

The kinds of things the publication should contain are the following:

- a description of what a data warehouse is
- a description of source systems feeding the warehouse
- how to use the data warehouse
- how to get help if there is a problem
- who is responsible for what
- the migration plan for the warehouse
- how warehouse data relates to operational data
- how to use warehouse data for DSS
- when not to add data to the warehouse
- what kind of data is not in the warehouse
- a guide to the metadata that is available
- what the system of record is

AUDITING AND THE DATA WAREHOUSE

An interesting issue that arises with data warehouses is whether auditing can be/should be done from the data warehouse. Auditing can be done from the data warehouse. There are a few examples of detailed audits being performed there. But there are many more reasons why auditing—even if it can be done from the data warehouse—should *not* be done from there. The primary reasons for not doing so are the following:

- Data that otherwise would not find its way into the warehouse suddenly has to be there.
- The timing of data entry into the warehouse changes dramatically when auditing capability is required.

- The backup and recovery restrictions for data warehouse change drastically when auditing capability is required.

In short, it is possible to do auditing from the data warehouse environment. However, the complications associated with auditing are such that it makes much more sense to do auditing elsewhere.

COST JUSTIFICATION

One of the interesting aspects of the data warehouse is that cost justification for the warehouse is normally not done on an a priori, return-on-investment basis. To do such an analysis requires that the benefits of a data warehouse be known prior to the building of the data warehouse.

In most cases, the real benefits of the data warehouse are not known or even anticipated at the moment of construction because the warehouse is used in a way entirely different from other data and systems built by information systems. The usage of the data warehouse occurs in a mode different from the rest of information processing—something like a "Tell me what I say I want, then I can tell you what I really want" mode. The DSS analyst really cannot say what the possibilities and potentials of the data warehouse are until the first iteration of the data warehouse is built and becomes available. Then, once the DSS analyst gets his/her hands on the warehouse, the DSS analyst can start to unlock the potential of DSS processing.

Thus it is that classical ROI techniques simply are not applicable to the data warehouse environment. Fortunately, data warehouses are built incrementally. The first iteration can be done quickly and for a relatively small amount of money. Once the first portion of the data warehouse is built and populated, the analyst can start to explore the possibilities. It is at this point that the analyst can start to justify the development costs of the warehouse.

As a rule of thumb, the first iteration of the data warehouse should be small enough to be able to be built and large enough to be meaningful.

For these reasons, the data warehouse is best built

- a small iteration at a time,
- with a direct feedback loop between the warehouse developer and the DSS analyst in place, and
- quickly.

In addition, these reasons explain why it is said that if the initial design of the data warehouse is 50 percent accurate as initially designed, then the design is a success. The feedback loop between the warehouse developer and the DSS analyst constantly are modifying the existing warehouse data and adding other data to the warehouse.

PURGING WAREHOUSE DATA

Data does not just pour into a data warehouse. It has its own life cycle within the warehouse as well. At some point in time, data is purged from the warehouse. The issue of purging data is one of the fundamental design issues that must not escape the data warehouse designer.

In some senses, data is not purged from the warehouse at all. It is simply rolled up to higher levels of summary. There are several ways in which data is purged or the detail of data is transformed.

- Data is added to a rolling summary file where detail is lost.
- Data is transferred to a bulk media from a high-performance media such as DASD.
- Data is actually purged from the system.
- Data is not transferred from one level of the architecture to another, such as from the operational level to the data warehouse level, and so forth.

There are, then, a variety of ways in which data is purged or otherwise transformed inside the data warehouse environment. The life cycle of data—including its purge or final archival dissemination—should be an active part of the design process for the data warehouse.

SUMMARY

In summary, this chapter described the data warehouse. The subject orientation, the time variant of each record of data, the linkage by a common key, have all been discussed.

The two most important design decisions that can be made are the granularity of data and the partitioning of data. For most organizations, a dual level of granularity makes the most sense.

Partitioning of data is done to break down the data in the data warehouse into small physical units. As a rule, partitioning is done at the application level rather than at the system level in the data warehouse.

3

Data Warehouse and Design

There are two major aspects to the building of the data warehouse—the design of the interface coming from operational systems and the design of the data warehouse itself. In a way, "design" is not an accurate description for what happens in the building of the data warehouse, which is constructed in a heuristic manner. First, one portion of data is populated. It is then used and scrutinized by the DSS analyst. Then, based on the feedback of the end user, the data is modified and/or other data is added to the data warehouse.

The feedback loop continues throughout the entire life of the data warehouse. It is a mistake to think that design approaches that have worked in the past will suffice in building the data warehouse. The requirements for the data warehouse CANNOT BE KNOWN until it is partially populated and being used by the DSS analyst. So, it cannot be designed in the same way that the classical requirements-driven system is designed. On the other hand, it is also a mistake to think that not anticipating requirements is a good idea. The answer lies somewhere in between.

BEGINNING WITH OPERATIONAL DATA

At the outset, there is operational data that is locked up in existing systems. It is a temptation to think that all there is to creating the data warehouse is extracting operational data and entering it into the data warehouse. Nothing could be further from the truth.

Figure 3.1 shows a simple depiction of pulling data from the existing systems environment over to the data warehouse.

We see here that multiple applications will contribute to the data warehouse.

There are a multitude of reasons why this figure is overly simplistic. The primary fault in thinking that building a data warehouse is merely an extraction process is that the data in the operational environment is unintegrated. Figure 3.2 shows the lack of integration that is normal in the existing systems environment.

When the different existing applications were constructed, there was no thought given to possible future integration of the applications. Each application had its own set of unique and private requirements, and there was no consideration of other applications during the development process. It is no surprise, then, that some data exist in many places with different names; some data are labelled the same in different places but are still the same; and

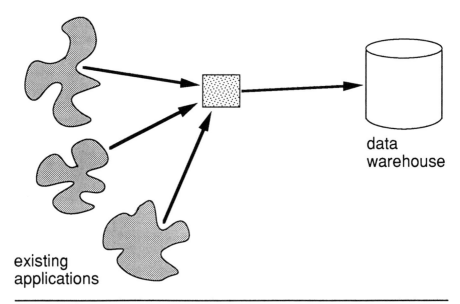

data
warehouse

existing
applications

Figure 3.1.   Moving data from the operational to the data warehouse environment is not as simple as mere extraction.

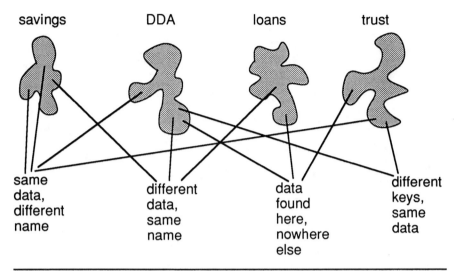

savings   DDA   loans   trust

same
data,
different
name

different
data,
same
name

data
found
here,
nowhere
else

different
keys,
same
data

Figure 3.2.   Data across the different applications are
terribly unintegrated.

some data are in the same place with the same name but reflect a different measurement of data, and so on. Trying to extract data from the many places it exists is a very complex problem.

This issue of lack of integration is the extract programmer's nightmare. There are a thousand and one details that have to be programmed just to bring the data from the operational environment properly, as illustrated in Figure 3.3.

As a simple example of lack of integration, data may not be encoded consistently, as shown by the encoding of gender. In one application, gender is encoded as "m/f". In another, it is encoded as "0/1". It really doesn't matter how gender is encoded in the data warehouse as long as it is encoded consistently. As data passes to the data warehouse, the different values must be correctly deciphered and recoded with the proper value.

As another example of the integration issues facing the developer, consider four applications that have the same field—pipeline. The field, however, is measured differently in each application. In one application, pipeline is measured in inches. In another, it is measured in centimeters, and so forth. It does not particularly

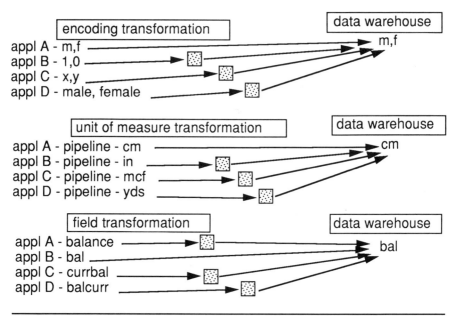

Figure 3.3.   In order to move data from the existing
systems environment to the data warehouse
environment properly, it must be integrated.

matter how pipeline is measured in the data warehouse, as long as
it is measured consistently.

Field transformation is another issue of integration. The same
field exists in four applications in four names. In order to transform
the data to the data warehouse properly, there must be a mapping
from the different source fields to the data warehouse fields.

These simple examples hardly scratch the surface of integration, and they are not complex in themselves. But when multiplied
by the thousands of existing systems and files, the issue of integration becomes very complex and burdensome.

But integration (or lack thereof) of existing systems is not the
only difficulty in the transformation of data from the operational,
existing systems environment to the data warehouse environment.
Another major problem is that of the efficiency of accessing existing
systems data. How does the program that scans existing systems
know whether a file has been scanned previously? When a file has

not been previously scanned? There is a lot of data in the existing systems environment and attempting to scan all of it every time a data warehouse scan is done is wasteful and unrealistic.

Performance of scanning existing files, then, is a major issue facing the data warehouse architect.

There are five common techniques used to limit the amount of data scanned, as shown in Figure 3.4.

The first technique is to scan data that has been timestamped. When an application happens to stamp the time of last change or update on a record, the data warehouse scan can run quite effi-

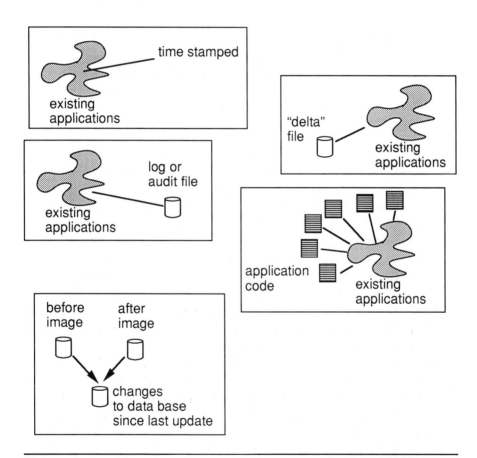

Figure 3.4.   How do you know what source data to scan? Do you scan every record every day? Every week?

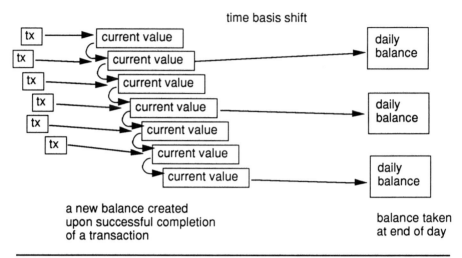

time basis shift

a new balance created
upon successful completion
of a transaction

balance taken
at end of day

Figure 3.5. A shift in time basis is required as data is moved over from the operational to the data warehouse environment.

ciently, because data with a date other than that applicable does not have to be touched. However, it usually is only by happenstance that existing data has been timestamped.

The second technique of limiting the data to be scanned for data warehouse extraction is to scan a "delta" file. A delta file is one that is created by an application that contains only the changes made to an application. When there is a delta file, the scan process is very efficient because data that is not a candidate for scanning is never touched. But not many applications build delta files.

The third technique is that of scanning an audit or log file. The log file or the audit file contain essentially the same data as a delta file. However, there are some major differences. Many times, operations protects the log files because they are needed in the recovery process. Computer operations is not particularly thrilled by having its log file used for something other than its primary purpose. Another difficulty with a log tape is that the internal format is built for systems purposes, not applications purposes. It may require a technological guru to interface the contents of data on the log tape. Another shortcoming of a log file is that it usually contains much more information than that desired by the data warehouse developer. Audit files have many of the same shortcomings as log files.

The fourth technique for managing the amount of data scanned as data warehouse extraction occurs is to modify application code. This is never a popular option, as much application code is old and fragile.

The last option (that in most respects is a hideous option and whose primary purpose is to convince people that there must be a better way) is that of rubbing a before and after image file together. In this option, a snapshot of a database is taken at the moment of extraction. When it comes time to do another extraction, another snapshot is taken. The two snapshots are serially compared to each other to determine the activity that has transpired. This approach is cumbersome, complex, and requires an inordinate amount of resources. It is simply a last resort.

But integration and performance are not the only major discrepancies that prevent a simple extract process from being used to construct the data warehouse. A third major difficulty is that of a time basis shift, as shown in Figure 3.5.

Existing operational data is almost always current value data. Current value data is data whose accuracy is valid as of the moment of access, and it can be updated. But data that goes into the data warehouse cannot be updated. This data must have an element of time attached to it. There needs to be a major shift in data, then, as data passes from the existing systems environment to the data warehouse environment.

Yet another major consideration when data is passed from the existing systems environment to the data warehouse environment is that of the need to manage the volume of data. Condensation of data needs to be done; otherwise, the volume of data in the data warehouse will grow out of control in rapid order. Condensation of data needs to begin at the moment of extraction. Figure 3.6 shows a simple form of condensation of data warehouse data.

DATA/PROCESS MODELS AND THE ARCHITECTED ENVIRONMENT

Before any attempt is made to apply conventional design techniques, the designer MUST understand the applicability and the limits of those techniques. Figure 3.7 shows the relationship between the levels of the architecture and the disciplines of data modelling and process modelling.

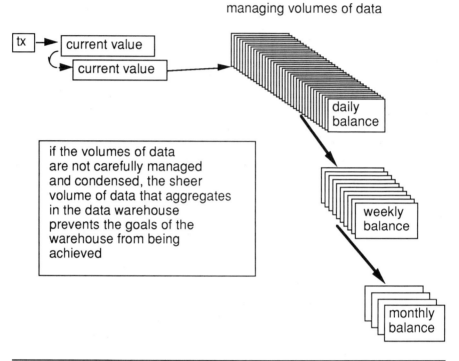

managing volumes of data

current value

current value

daily balance

weekly balance

monthly balance

if the volumes of data are not carefully managed and condensed, the sheer volume of data that aggregates in the data warehouse prevents the goals of the warehouse from being achieved

Figure 3.6.   Condensation of data is a vital factor in the managing of warehouse data.

Figure 3.7 shows that the process model applies to ONLY the operational environment. The data model applies to both the operational environment and the data warehouse environment. Trying to use a data or process model in the wrong place will produce nothing but frustration.

Data models will be discussed in depth later. What is a process model? A process model typically consists of the following (in whole or in part):

- a functional decomposition
- a context level zero diagram
- a data flow diagram
- a structure chart
- a state transition diagram

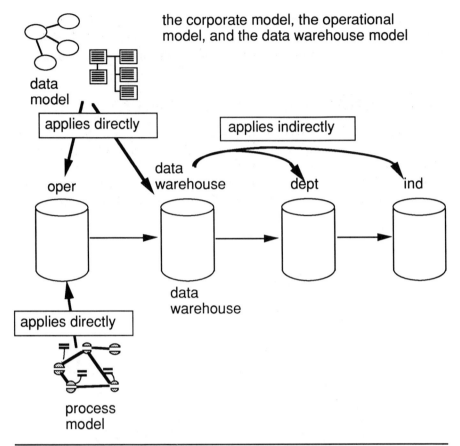

the corporate model, the operational
model, and the data warehouse model

Figure 3.7.   How the different types of models apply to the
architected environment.

- a HIPO chart
- pseudocode

There are many contexts and many environments where a
process model is invaluable. But in building the data warehouse, a
process model is a hindrance. The process model is requirements
based. This assumes that there is a set of requirements that is
known—a priori—before the details of the design are established.
In dealing with processes such an assumption can be made. But

those assumptions do not hold for the data warehouse. Indeed, many development tools have the same orientation, such as CASE tools, and as such are not applicable to the data warehouse environment.

DATA WAREHOUSE AND DATA MODELS

The data model is shown as being applicable to both the existing systems environment and the data warehouse environment. A more lucid explanation is depicted in Figure 3.8.

Figure 3.8 shows that there is an overall corporate data model that has been constructed with no regard for a distinction between

Figure 3.8. How the different levels of modelling relate.

existing, operational systems and data warehouse. The corporate data model contains only primitive data.

In order to construct a separate existing data model, the beginning point is the corporate model, as shown. However, performance factors are added in to the corporate data model as the model is transported to the existing systems environment. All in all, very few changes are made to the corporate data model as it is used operationally.

However, there are a fair number of changes that are made to the corporate data model as it is applied to the data warehouse. The first thing that is done is that data that is used purely in the operational environment is removed. Next, the key structures of the corporate data model are enhanced with an element of time. Derived data is added to the corporate data model where the derived data is publicly used and calculated once, not repeatedly. And, finally, data relationships in the operational environment are turned into "artifacts" in the data warehouse.

There is, then, a common genesis of data models. Using an analogy, the corporate data model is Adam, the operational data model is Cain, and the data warehouse data model is Abel. They are all from the same lineage, and, at the same time, they are all different.

The Data Model

(Other books have been written on data modelling. There are a wide number of approaches to choose from. Any number of the approaches can be used successfully in the building of a data warehouse. The approach that will be discussed here, in a summary fashion, can be further explored in the book, *Practical Information Engineering*, QED.)

There are three levels of data modelling: high level of modelling (called the ERD, entity relationship level), midlevel of modelling (called the dis, data item set), and the low level of modelling (called the "physical model").

The high level of modelling features entities and relationships, as shown in Figure 3.9.

The name of the entity is surrounded by an oval. Relationships between entities are depicted with arrows. The direction and number of the arrowheads indicate the cardinality of the relationship,

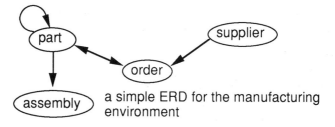

a simple ERD for the manufacturing environment

Figure 3.9.   Representing entities and relationships.

and only direct relationships are indicated. In doing so, transitive dependencies are minimized.

The entities that are shown in the ERD level are at the highest level of abstraction. The determination of what entities belong in the scope of the model and what entities do not is determined by what is termed the "scope of integration," as shown in Figure 3.10.

The scope of integration defines the boundaries of the data model and needs to be defined before the modelling process commences. The scope is agreed upon by the modeller, management and the ultimate user of the system. If the scope is not predetermined, there is the great chance that the modelling process will continue on forever. The definition of the scope of integration should be written in no more than five pages and written in language understandable to the businessperson.

The corporate ERD is a composite of many individual ERDs that reflect the different views of people across the corporation, as seen in Figure 3.11.

Figure 3.11 shows that separate high-level data models have

Figure 3.10.   The scope of integration determines what portion of the enterprise will be reflected in the data model.

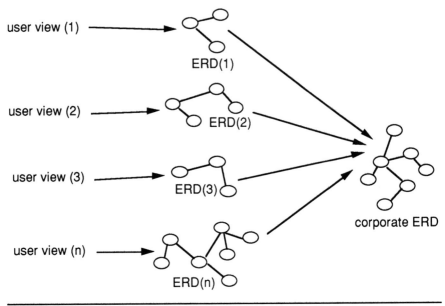

Figure 3.11.   The construction of the corporate ERD from
the different user view ERDs.

been created for different communities within the corporation.
Collectively they comprise the corporate ERD.

The community ERDs are created by means of user view sessions, which are interview sessions with the appropriate personnel
in the various departments.

The Midlevel Data Model

After the high-level data model is created, the next level is established—the midlevel model, or the dis. For each major subject area,
or entity, identified in the high-level data model, a midlevel model
is created, as seen in Figure 3.12.

In the figure, the high-level data model has identified four
entities, or major subject areas. Each of the major subject areas is
subsequently developed into its own midlevel model.

Interestingly, only very rarely are all of the midlevel models
developed at once. The midlevel data model for one major subject

Figure 3.12.   Each entity in the ERD is further defined by its own dis.

area is expanded, then the midlevel model is fleshed out, and so forth.

The constructs of data modelling that are found at the midlevel modelling are shown in Figure 3.13.

There are four basic constructs for the midlevel model.

- a primary grouping of data
- a secondary grouping of data
- a connector, signifying the relationships of data between major subject areas
- "type of" data

The primary grouping exists once, and only once, for each major subject area. It holds attributes that exist only once for each major subject area. As with all groupings of data, the primary grouping of data contains attributes and keys.

The secondary grouping of data holds data attributes that can exist multiple times for each major subject area. The secondary grouping is indicated by a line emanating downward from the pri-

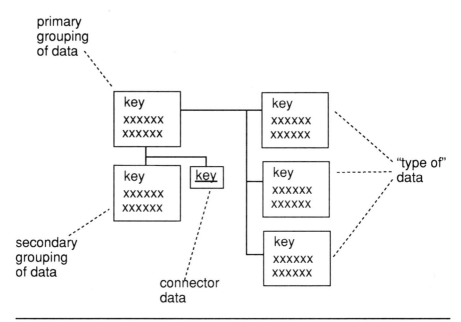

Figure 3.13.   The four constructs that make up the mid level data model:

- the primary grouping of data
- the secondary grouping of data
- connector data
- "type of" data

mary grouping of data. There may be as many secondary groupings as there are distinct groups of data that can occur multiple times.

The third construct is the connector. The connector relates data from one grouping to another grouping of data. A relationship identified at the ERD level results in an acknowledgment at the dis level. The convention used to indicate a connector is an underlining of a foreign key.

The fourth construct in the data model is that of "type of" data. "Type of" data is indicated by a line leading to the right of a grouping of data. The grouping of data to the left is the super type. The grouping of data to the right is the sub-type of data.

These four data modelling constructs are used to identify the

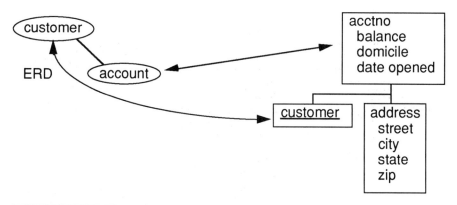

Figure 3.14.   The relationships identified in the ERD are reflected by connectors in the dis. Note that only one connector—from acctno to customer—is shown in this diagram. In reality, another connector from customer to acctno would be shown elsewhere in the dis for customer.

attributes of data in a data model and the relationship between those attributes.

When a relationship is identified at the ERD level, it is manifested by a pair of connector relationships at the dis level. Figure 3.14 shows one of those pairs.

At the ERD, a relationship between customer and account has been identified. At the dis level for account, there exists a connector beneath account. This indicates that an account may have multiple customers attached to it. Not shown is the corresponding relationship beneath the customer in the customer dis. In the customer dis, there will be a connector to account, indicating that a customer can have an account or accounts.

As an example of what a full-blown dis might look like, consider the example shown in Figure 3.15.

In Figure 3.15 there is a dis for an account for a financial institute. All of the different constructs are shown in the dis.

Of particular interest is the case where a grouping of data has two "type of" lines emanating from it, as seen in Figure 3.16.

The two lines leading to the right indicate that there are two "type of" criteria. One type of criteria is by activity type—either a

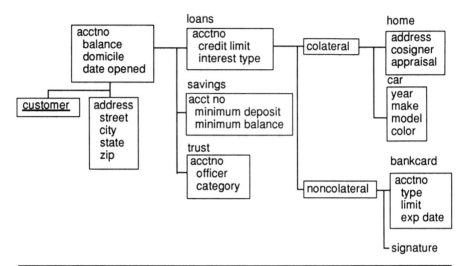

Figure 3.15.   An expanded dis showing the different types of loans that a bank may support.

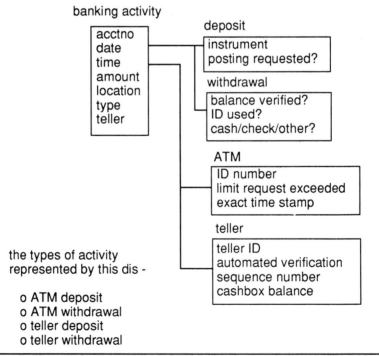

Figure 3.16.   A dis showing different subcategorization criteria.

deposit or a withdrawal. The other line indicates another type—either an ATM activity or a teller activity. Collectively, the two types of activity encompass the following transactions:

- ATM deposit
- ATM withdrawal
- teller deposit
- teller withdrawal

Another feature of the diagram is that all common data is to the left, and all unique data is to the right. For example, the attributes date and time are common to all transactions. But cashbox balance is common to only teller activity.

The relationship between the data model and physical tables that result from the data model is shown in Figure 3.17.

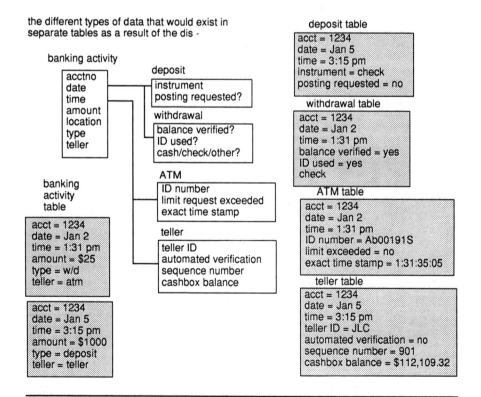

Figure 3.17. The table entries that are represented by the two transactions.

In general, each grouping of data in the data model results in a table being defined in the database design process. Assuming that to be the case, two transactions result in several table entries, as seen in the figure. The physical table entries that resulted came from the following two transactions:

- an ATM withdrawal that occurred at 1:31 p.m. on January 2, and
- a teller deposit that occurred at 3:15 p.m. on January 5.

The two transactions caused six entries in five separate tables to be generated.

Like the corporate ERD that is created from different ERDs reflecting the community of users, the corporate dis is created from multiple dises, as illustrated by Figure 3.18.

Figure 3.18 shows that when the interviews or JAD sessions are done for a particular user, a dis, as well as an ERD, is created. The parochial dis is then merged with all other dises to form the corporate view of a dis.

The Physical Data Model

The physical data model is created from the midlevel data model merely by extending the midlevel data model to include keys and physical characteristics of the model. At this point, the physical data model looks like a series of tables, sometimes called relational tables.

It is a temptation to say that the tables are ready to be cast into the concrete of physical database design at this moment. However, one last design step remains—factoring in the performance characteristics.

In the case of the data warehouse, the first step in the factoring of performance characteristics means deciding on the granularity and partitioning of the data. This step must be done.

Of course, the key structure is changed to add the element of time, to which each unit of data is relevant.

After granularity and partitioning are factored in, a variety of other physical design activities are embedded into the design. These other physical design considerations are outlined in Figure 3.19.

Figure 3.18.   The corporate dis is made up of the dis
created as a result of each user view session.

At the heart of the physical design considerations is the usage of physical I/O (input/output). Physical I/O is the activity that brings data into the computer from storage or sends data to storage from the computer. Figure 3.20 shows a simple case of I/O.

Data is transferred to and from the computer to storage in terms of blocks. The reason that the I/O event is so important to perfor-

data
model

- performance -
  - arrays of data
  - merging tables
  - selective redundancy
  - further separation of data
  - derived data
  - preformatting, preallocation
  - relationship artifacts
  - prejoining tables

physical
database
design

Figure 3.19. Getting good performance out of the data warehouse environment.

mance is that the transfer of data to and from storage to the computer occurs at roughly two to three orders of magnitude slower than the speeds at which the computer runs. The computer runs internally in terms of nanosecond speed. Transfer of data to and from storage occurs in terms of milliseconds. Thus, physical I/O is the main impediment to performance.

The job of the data warehouse designer is to physically organize data so that the maximum number of records is returned that will be used from the execution of a physical I/O. (Note: This is not an issue of blindly transferring a large number of records from DASD

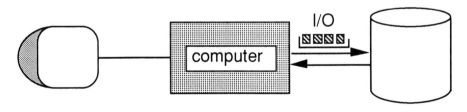

I/O

computer

Figure 3.20. Getting the most out of the physical I/Os that have to be done.

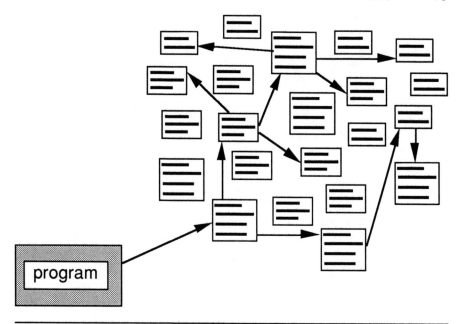

Figure 3.21.   When there are many tables, much I/O is
required for dynamic interconnectability.

to main storage. This is a more sophisticated issue of transferring a
bulk of records that have a high probability of being accessed.)

For example, suppose a programmer must fetch five records. If
those records are organized into different blocks of data on storage,
then five I/Os will be required. But if the designer can anticipate
that the records will be needed as a group and can physically
juxtapose those records into the same physical block, then only one
I/O will be required, thus making the program run much more
efficiently.

There is another mitigating factor about physical placement of
data in the data warehouse, and that factor is that data in the
warehouse normally are not updated. This frees the designer to use
physical design techniques that otherwise would not be acceptable
if data were regularly updated.

NORMALIZATION/DENORMALIZATION

The output of the data model process is a series of tables, each of which contains keys and attributes. The normal output of the data model process is LOTS of tables, each of which contains only a modicum of data.

While there is nothing wrong—per se—with lots of little tables, from a performance perspective there is a problem. Consider the work the program has to do in order to interconnect the tables dynamically, as shown in Figure 3.21.

In Figure 3.21, a program goes into execution. First, one table is accessed, then another table is accessed. In order to successfully execute, the program has to jump around many tables. Each time the program jumps from one table to the next, I/O is consumed. I/O is consumed both in terms of accessing the data and in terms of accessing the index to find the data. If there were only one or two programs that had to pay the price of I/O, there would be no problem. But when ALL programs have to pay a stiff price for I/O, then performance in general suffers, and that is precisely what happens when many small tables, each containing a limited amount of data, are created as a physical design.

A more rational approach is to merge the tables together so that only a minimum of I/O is consumed, as seen in Figure 3.22.

Figure 3.22 shows that the many small tables have been physically merged together. In doing so, the same program operates as before, only now it needs much less I/O to accomplish the same task.

The question, then, becomes what is a sane strategy to merge the tables together so that the maximum benefit is derived? It is in answering this question that the physical database designer earns his/her reward.

But merging tables together is only one design technique that can save I/O. Another very useful technique is that of creating an array of data, as seen in Figure 3.23.

In Figure 3.23, there is data that are normalized so that each occurrence of a sequence of data resides in a different physical location. Retrieving each occurrence, n, n + 1, n + 2, . . . , requires a physical I/O in order to get the data.

If the data were placed in a single row in an array, then a single I/O would suffice to retrieve the data, as shown at the bottom of the figure.

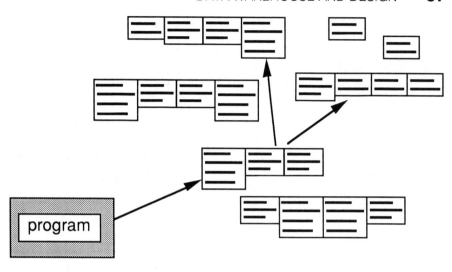

Figure 3.22. When tables are physically merged, much less I/O is required.

Of course, it does not make sense to create an array of data in every case. Only when there are a stable number of occurrences, where the data is accessed in sequence, where the data is created and/or updated in a statistically well-behaved sequence, and so forth, does it make sense to create an array of data.

Interestingly, in the data warehouse, these circumstances occur regularly because of the time-based orientation of the data. Data warehouse data is always relevant to some moment in time, and units of time occur with great regularity. In the data warehouse, creating an array by month, for example, is a very easy, natural thing to do.

Another important design technique that is especially relevant to the data warehouse environment is that of the deliberate introduction of redundant data. Figure 3.24 shows an example where the deliberate introduction of redundant data pays a big dividend.

In the top of the figure, the field—description—is normalized and exists nonredundantly. In doing so, all processes that need to see the description of a part have to access the base parts table. The access of the data is very expensive, although the update of the data is optimal.

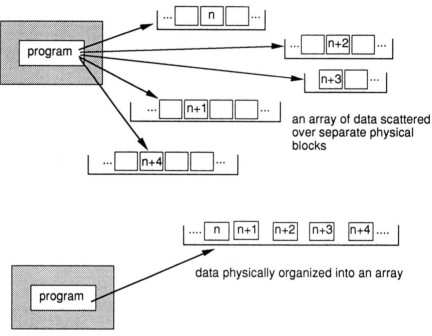

Figure 3.23. Under the right circumstances, creating arrays of data can save considerable resources.

In the bottom of the figure, the data element—description—has been deliberately placed in the many tables where it is likely to be used. In doing so, the access of data is more efficient, and the update of data is not optimal. However, for data that is widely used (such as description), and for data that is stable (such as description), there is little reason to worry about update. In particular, in the data warehouse environment, there is no concern whatsoever for update.

Another useful technique is that of the further separation of data when there is a wide disparity in the probability of access. Figure 3.25 shows such a case.

In Figure 3.25, concerning a bank account, the domicile of the account and the data opened for the account are normalized together with the balance of the account. Yet, the balance of the account has a very different probability of access than do the other

selective use of redundancy

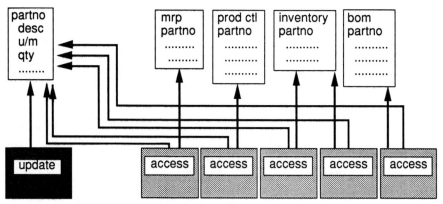

description is nonredundant and is used frequently
but is seldom updated

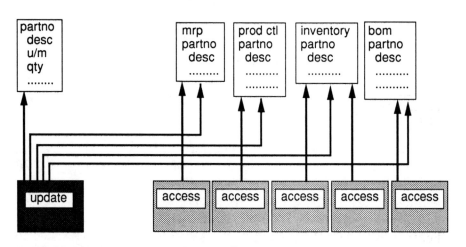

Figure 3.24.   Description is redundantly spread over the
many places it is used. It must be updated in
many places when it changes. But it seldom, if
ever, changes.

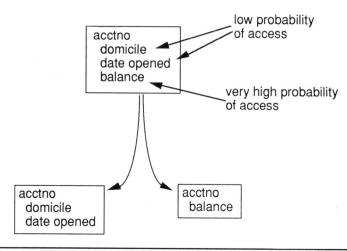

Figure 3.25. Further separation of data based on a wide disparity in the probability of access.

two data elements. The balance of an account is VERY popular, while the other data are hardly ever accessed. In order to make I/O more efficient and to more compactly store the data, it makes sense to further reduce the normalized table into two separate tables, as shown.

Occasionally, the introduction of derived data into the physical database design can reduce the amount of I/O needed. Figure 3.26 shows such a case.

In Figure 3.26, a program accesses payroll data regularly in order to calculate the annual pay and taxes that have been paid. If the program is run regularly and at the year's end, it makes sense to create fields of data to store the calculated data. The data has only to be calculated once. Then all future requirements can merely access the calculated field. This approach has another advantage in that once the field is calculated, it will not have to be calculated again, eliminating the risk of faulty algorithms from incorrect evaluations.

One of the most innovative techniques in building a data warehouse is what can be termed a "creative" index, or a creative profile (a term coined by Les Moore). Figure 3.27 shows an example of a creative index.

A creative index is created as data is passed from the operaintroducing derived data

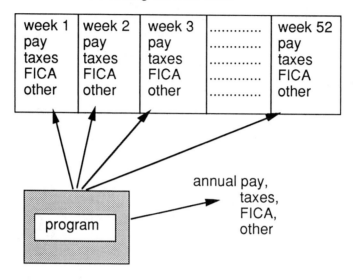

Figure 3.26. Derived data, calculated once, then forever available.

tional environment to the data warehouse environment. Since each unit of data has to be handled in any case, it requires very little overhead to calculate or create an index at this point.

The creative index does a profile on items of interest to the end user, such as the largest purchases, the most inactive accounts, the latest shipments, and so on. If the requirements that might be of interest to management can be anticipated (admittedly, they cannot in every case), then at the time of passing data to the data warehouse, it makes sense to build a creative index.

A final design technique that the data warehouse designer needs to be aware of is the management of referential integrity in

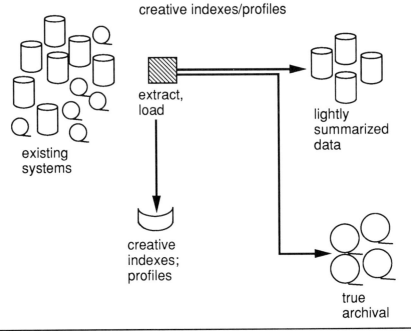

creative indexes/profiles

extract, load

existing systems

lightly summarized data

creative indexes; profiles

true archival

Figure 3.27.   Examples of creative indexes:

- The top ten customers in volume are—
- The average transaction value for this extract was $nnn.nn.
- The largest transaction was $nnn.nn.
- The number of customers who showed activity without purchasing was nn.

the data warehouse environment. Figure 3.28 shows that referential integrity appears as "artifacts" of relationships in the data warehouse environment.

In the operational environment, referential integrity appears as a dynamic link among tables of data. But the volume of data in a data warehouse, the fact that the data warehouse is not updated, and the fact that the data warehouse represents data over time, and relationships do not stay static over time, mandates that a different approach be taken to referential integrity in the data warehouse environment. In a word, relationships of data are repredata warehouse and referential integrity

in operational systems, the relationships
between databases are handled by referential
integrity

But, in the data warehouse environment
  o there is much more data than in the operational
    environment
  o the data once in the warehouse doesn't change
  o there is a need to represent more than one business
    rule over time
  o data purges in the warehouse are not tightly
    coordinated

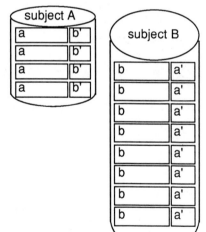

artifacts in the data warehouse
environment
  o can be managed
    independently
  o are very efficient to
    access
  o do not require update

Figure 3.28.   Referential integrity in the data warehouse
environment.

sented by an artifact in the data warehouse environment. This means that some data will be duplicated, and some data will be deleted when other data are still in the warehouse. In any case, trying to replicate referential integrity in the data warehouse environment is a patently incorrect approach.

METADATA

An important aspect of the data warehouse environment is that of metadata. Metadata is data about data. Metadata has been a part of the information processing milieu for as long as there have been programs and data. But it is in the world of data warehouses that metadata takes on a new level of importance. It is with metadata that the most effective use of the data warehouse is made. Metadata allows the end user/DSS analyst to navigate through the possibilities.

Metadata sits above the warehouse and keeps track of what is where in the warehouse. Typically, the things the metadata store tracks are

- the structure of data as known to the programmer,
- the structure of data as known to the DSS analyst,
- the source data feeding the data warehouse,
- the transformation of data as it passes into the data warehouse,
- the data model,
- the relation between the data model and the data warehouse, and
- the history of extracts.

SUMMARY

The design of the data warehouse begins with the data model. The corporate data model is used for the design of the operational environment, and a variation of the corporate data model is used for the data warehouse. The data warehouse is constructed in an iterative fashion. Requirements for the data warehouse CANNOT be known a priori. The construction of the data warehouse is under a development life cycle completely different from that of classical operational systems.

The primary concern of the data warehouse developer is that of managing volume. To that end, the issues of granularity and partitioning of data are the two most important issues of database design. There are, however, many other physical design issues, most of which center around the efficiency of access of data.

4

Granularity in the Data Warehouse

The single most important design issue facing the data warehouse developer is that of determining the granularity in the data warehouse. When the granularity of a data warehouse is properly set, the remaining aspects of design and implementation flow smoothly; when it has not been set, every other aspect is awkward.

The tradeoff in choosing the right levels of granularity—as discussed earlier—centers around managing the volume of data and storing data at such a high level of granularity that detailed usage of the data cannot be made.

RAW ESTIMATES

The starting point for determining the appropriate level of granularity is to do a raw estimate of the number of rows of data and the DASD that will be in the data warehouse. Admittedly, in the best of circumstances, only an estimate can be made. But all that is required at the inception of building the warehouse is an order of magnitude estimate in any case.

There is an algorithmic path to calculating the space occupied by a data warehouse, as shown in Figure 4.1.

The first step is to identify all the tables that will be built. Next,

```
┌─────────────────────────────────────────────────────────────┐
│ estimating rows/space for the warehouse environment -        │
└─────────────────────────────────────────────────────────────┘
```

1. for each known table -
   how big is a row (in bytes) -
      - biggest estimate -
      - smallest estimate -
   for the 1-year horizon -
      what is the maximum number of rows possible? -
      what is the minimum number of rows possible? -
   for the 5-year horizon -
      what is the maximum number of rows possible? -
      what is the minimum number of rows possible? -
   for each key of the table -
      what is the size of the key (in bytes) -
   total maximum 1-year space = biggest row x 1-year max rows
   total minimum 1-year space = smallest row x 1-year min rows
    plus index space

2. repeat (1) for all known tables

Figure 4.1.   Space/rows calculations.

estimate the size of the row in each table. It is likely that the exact size will not be known. A lower-bound estimate and an upper-bound estimate are sufficient.

Next, on the one-year horizon, estimate the maximum number of rows and the minimum number of rows in the table. This estimate is the one that gives the designer the greatest problem. If the table is for customers, use today's estimate of customers, factoring in business conditions and the corporate business plan. If there is no existing business today, estimate total market multiplied by expected market share. If the market share is unpredictable, use an estimate of what a competitor has achieved. In short, start with a reasonable estimate of customers gathered from one or more sources.

If the warehouse is to contain activity, go from estimated number of customers to estimated activity per unit of time. Again, the same logic is used, looking at current business profiles, a competitor's profile, economist projections, etc.

Once the estimate of number of units of data in the data warehouse is made (using a high and a low projection), the estimation process is repeated, except for the five-year horizon, not the one-year horizon.

After the raw data projections are made, the index data space projections are calculated. For each table—for each key in the table—identify the length of the key and whether the key will exist for each entry in the primary table.

Now the high and low numbers for the occurrences of rows in the tables are multiplied respectively by the maximum and minimum lengths of data. In addition, the number of index entries is multiplied by the length of the key and added to the total amount of data.

INPUT INTO THE PLANNING PROCESS

The estimate of rows and DASD then serves as input into the planning process, as shown by Figure 4.2.

At the point that the estimates are made, accuracy is really only important to the order of magnitude.

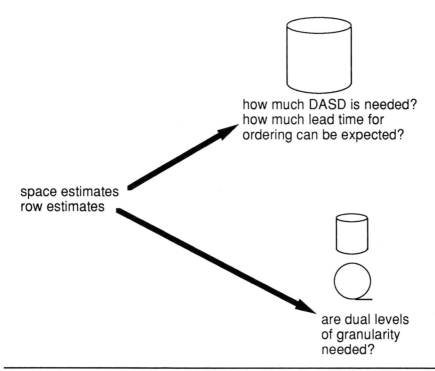

how much DASD is needed?
how much lead time for
ordering can be expected?

space estimates
row estimates

are dual levels
of granularity
needed?

Figure 4.2.   Using the output of the space estimates.

DUAL OR SINGULAR LEVELS OF GRANULARITY?

Once the estimates are made, the next step is to compare the total number of rows in the warehouse environment to the charts shown in Figure 4.3.

The chart shown in Figure 4.3 shows that depending on how many total rows there will be in the warehouse environment, different approaches to design and development will have to be made. On the one-year horizon, if there will be less than 10,000 rows, then practically any design and implementation will work. For the one-year horizon, if there will be 100,000 total rows or less, then design must be done carefully. If there will be more than 1,000,000 rows in total in the first year, dual levels of granularity will be called for. And if the total number of rows in the data warehouse environment is to exceed 10,000,000 rows, dual levels of granularity will be mandated, and a very careful design and implementation will be required.

On the five-year horizon, the totals shift by about an order of magnitude. The theory is that after five years

- there will be more expertise available in managing the data warehouse volumes of data,
- hardware costs will have dropped to some extent,
- more powerful software tools will be available, and
- the end user will be more sophisticated.

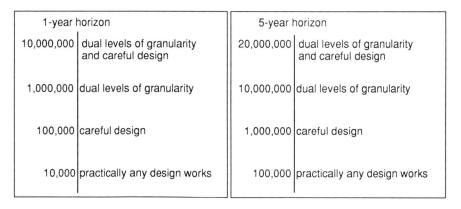

1-year horizon		5-year horizon	
10,000,000	dual levels of granularity and careful design	20,000,000	dual levels of granularity and careful design
1,000,000	dual levels of granularity	10,000,000	dual levels of granularity
100,000	careful design	1,000,000	careful design
10,000	practically any design works	100,000	practically any design works

Figure 4.3.   The thresholds of granularity.

All of these factors point to a different volume of data that can be managed over a long period of time.

An interesting point is that the total bytes used in the warehouse have little to do with the design and granularity issues. For the most part, that is the case. In other words, it does not matter whether the record is 25 bytes long or 250 bytes long. The chart shown in Figure 4.3 still applies. The reason has as much to do with the indexing of data as anything else. The same number of index entries is required regardless of the size of the record being indexed. Only under exceptional circumstances does the actual size of the record being indexed play a role in determining whether the data warehouse should contain dual levels of granularity.

WHAT THE LEVELS OF GRANULARITY WILL BE

Once the simple analysis is done (and in truth, most companies discover that they need dual levels of granularity), the next step is to determine exactly what the level of granularity is to be. The starting point is common sense and a certain amount of intuition. Creating a lightly summarized level of data that is at a very low level of detail doesn't make sense because too many resources will be required to process the data. Creating a lightly summarized level of detail that is too high means that much analysis will have to be done at the true archival level. So the first cut at the lightly summarized level of granularity is to make an educated guess.

But an educated guess is only the starting point. To refine the guess, a certain amount of iterative analysis is needed, as shown in Figure 4.4.

In order to determine the proper level of granularity for the lightly summarized data, the only real way to make the determination is to put the data in front of the end user. It is only after the end user has actually seen the data that a definitive answer can be given. Figure 4.4 shows the iterative loop that must transpire.

SOME FEEDBACK LOOP TECHNIQUES

The following are some techniques that apply to making the feedback loop a harmonious one:

RULE OF THUMB -
IF 50% OF THE FIRST ITERATION OF DESIGN IS CORRECT,
THE DESIGN EFFORT HAS BEEN A SUCCESS

o building very small subsets quickly and carefully listening to feedback
o prototyping
o looking at what other people have done
o working with an experienced user
o looking at what the organization has now
o JAD sessions with simulated output

Figure 4.4.   Now that I see what can be done, I can tell you
what would really be useful.

- Build the first parts of the data warehouse in very small, very fast steps, and carefully listen to the end users' comments. Be prepared to make adjustments quickly.
- Use prototyping if such a tool is available, and allow the feedback loop to function using observations gleaned from the prototype.
- Look at how other people have built their levels of granularity and learn from their experience.
- Go through the feedback process with an experienced user who is aware of the process that is occurring. Under no circumstances keep your users in the dark as to the dynamics of the feedback loop.
- Look at whatever the organization has now that appears to be working.
- Execute JAD sessions and simulate the output in order to achieve the desired feedback.

There are many ways that granularity of data can be raised. Some of them are the following:

- Summarize data from the source as it goes into the target.
- Average or otherwise calculate data as it goes into the target.
- Push highest/lowest set values into the target.
- Push only data that is obviously needed into the target.
- Use conditional logic to select only a subset of records to go into the target.

There are no limits as to how data may be lightly summarized. The limitation is in the mind of the designer.

There is one important point. In classical requirements systems development, it is unwise to proceed until the vast majority of the requirements are identified. But in building the data warehouse, it is unwise to not proceed if at least half of the requirements for the data warehouse are identified. In other words, if in building the data warehouse the developer waits until many requirements are identified, then the warehouse will never be built. It is vitally important that the feedback loop with the DSS analyst be initiated as soon as possible.

LEVELS OF GRANULARITY—BANKING ENVIRONMENT

Consider the simple data structures shown in Figure 4.5 for a banking/financial environment.

To the left—at the operational level—is operational data. The details of banking transactions are found there. Sixty days' worth of activity are stored in the operational online environment.

In the lightly summarized level of processing—shown to the right of the operational data—are up to 10 years' history of activities. The activities for a given account for a given month are stored in the lightly summarized portion of the data warehouse. While there are many records here, they are much more compact than the source records. Much less DASD and many fewer rows are found in the lightly summarized level of data.

Of course, there is the true archival level of data, in which every detailed record is stored. The true archival level of data are stored on

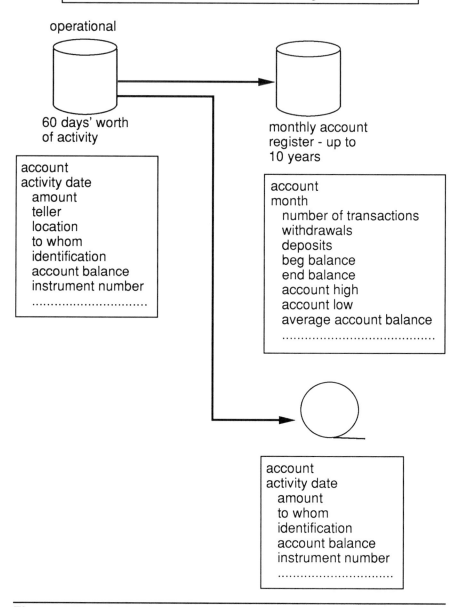

Figure 4.5.   A simple example of dual levels of granularity in the banking environment.

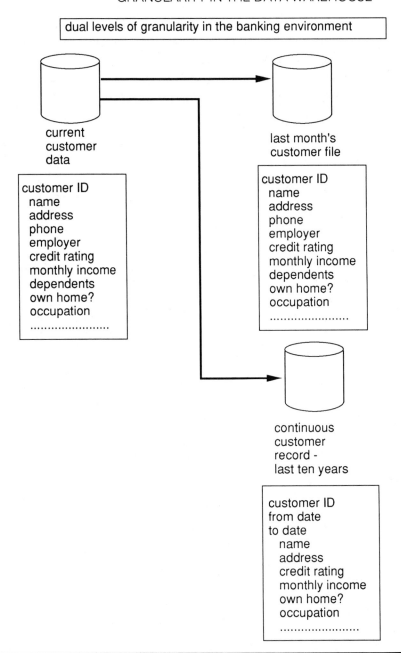

dual levels of granularity in the banking environment

current
customer
data

customer ID
  name
  address
  phone
  employer
  credit rating
  monthly income
  dependents
  own home?
  occupation
  ....

last month's
customer file

customer ID
  name
  address
  phone
  employer
  credit rating
  monthly income
  dependents
  own home?
  occupation
  ....

continuous
customer
record -
last ten years

customer ID
from date
to date
  name
  address
  credit rating
  monthly income
  own home?
  occupation
  ....

Figure 4.6.   Another form of dual levels of granularity in the
banking environment.

a medium suited to bulk management of data. Note that not all fields of data are transported to the true archival level. Only those fields of data needed for legal reasons, informational reasons, etc., are stored. The data that has further use, even in an archival mode, are purged from the system as data are passed to the true archival level.

The true archival environment can be held in a single medium, such as magnetic tape, which is cheap for storage and expensive for access. However, it is entirely possible to store a small part of the true archival level of data online, when there is a probability that the data might be needed. For example, a bank might store the most recent 30 days of activities online. The last 30 days is true archival data, but it is still online. At the end of the 30-day period, the data is sent to magnetic tape, and space is made available for the next 30 days' worth of true archival data.

Now consider another example of data in an architected environment in the banking/financial environment, as shown by Figure 4.6.

Figure 4.6 shows customer records spread across the environment. In the operational environment is shown current value data whose content is accurate as of the moment of usage. The data that exist at the light level of summarization are the same data (in terms of definition of data) but are taken as a snapshot once a month.

Where the customer data are kept over a long span of time—for the past 10 years—a continuous file is created from the monthly files. In such a fashion the history of a customer can be tracked over a lengthy period of time.

Moving to another industry—manufacturing—the architected environment is shown in Figure 4.7.

At the operational level is the record of manufacture upon the completion of an assembly for a given lot of parts. Throughout the day there are many records that aggregate as the assembly process runs.

The light level of summarization contains two tables—one for all the activities for a part summarized by day, and another by assembly activity by part. The parts cumulative production table contains data up to 90 days. The assembly record contains a limited amount of data on the production activity summarized by date.

The true archival environment contains a detailed record of each manufacture activity. However, as in the case of a bank, only those

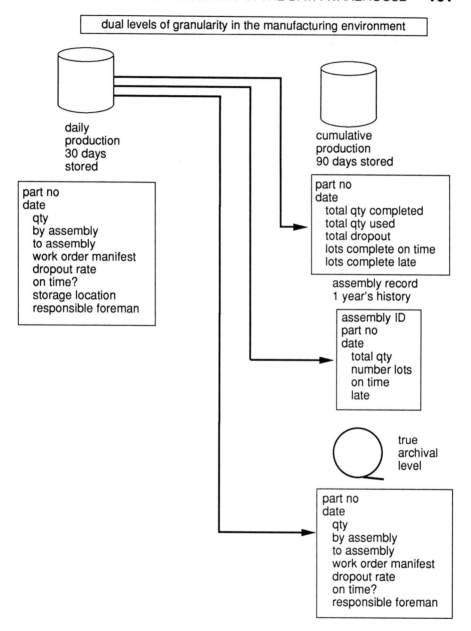

Figure 4.7.   Some of the different levels of granularity in a manufacturing environment.

fields that will be needed later are stored (Actually, those fields that have a reasonable probability of being needed later are stored.)

Another example of data warehouse granularity in the manufacturing environment is shown in Figure 4.8.

In Figure 4.8, there is an active order file in the operational environment. All orders that need activity are stored there. In the data warehouse is stored up to 10 years' worth of order history. The order history is keyed on the primary key and several secondary keys. Only the data that will be needed for future analysis is stored in the warehouse.

The volume of orders was so small that going to a true archival level was not necessary. Of course, should there start to be a plethora of orders, then it may well be necessary to go to a lower level of granularity.

Showing another adaptation of a shift in granularity is the data

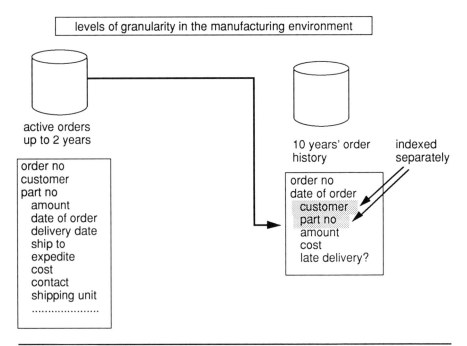

Figure 4.8. There are (relatively) so few order records that there is no need for a dual level of granularity.

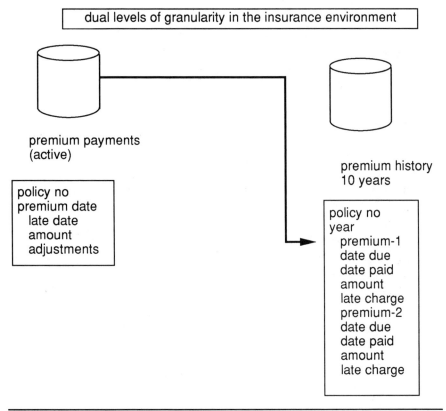

dual levels of granularity in the insurance environment

premium payments
(active)

premium history
10 years

policy no
premium date
  late date
  amount
  adjustments

policy no
year
  premium-1
  date due
  date paid
  amount
  late charge
  premium-2
  date due
  date paid
  amount
  late charge

Figure 4.9.   Because of the low volume of premiums, there is
no need for dual levels of granularity, and
because of the regularity of premium billing, there
is the opportunity to create an array of data.

in the architected environment of an insurance company, shown in
Figure 4.9.

In Figure 4.9, premium payment information is collected in an
active file. Then, after a period of time, the information is passed to
the data warehouse. Because there is only a relatively small amount
of data, there is no need for dual levels of granularity. However,
because of the regularity of premium payments, the payments are
stored as part of an array in the warehouse.

As another example of architecture in the insurance environment,
consider the insurance claims information shown in Figure 4.10.

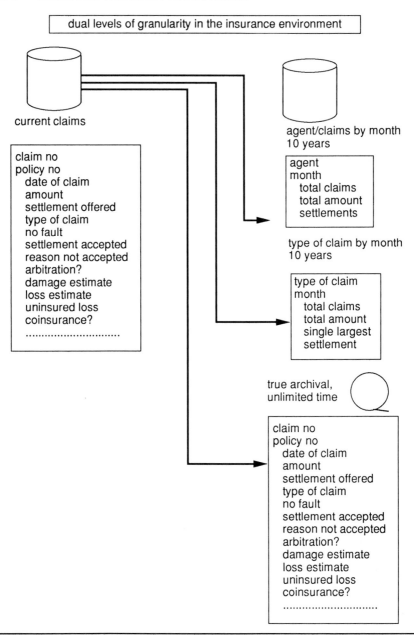

dual levels of granularity in the insurance environment

current claims

claim no
policy no
  date of claim
  amount
  settlement offered
  type of claim
  no fault
  settlement accepted
  reason not accepted
  arbitration?
  damage estimate
  loss estimate
  uninsured loss
  coinsurance?
  ....

agent/claims by month
10 years

agent
month
  total claims
  total amount
  settlements

type of claim by month
10 years

type of claim
month
  total claims
  total amount
  single largest
  settlement

true archival,
unlimited time

claim no
policy no
  date of claim
  amount
  settlement offered
  type of claim
  no fault
  settlement accepted
  reason not accepted
  arbitration?
  damage estimate
  loss estimate
  uninsured loss
  coinsurance?
  ....

Figure 4.10. Claims information is summarized on other than the primary key in the lightly summarized part of the warehouse. Claim information must be kept indefinitely in the true archival portion of the architecture.

In the current claims system (the operational part of the environment), much detailed information is stored about claims. When a claim is settled (or when it is determined that a claim is not going to be settled), or when enough time passes that the claim is still pending, the claim information passes over to the data warehouse. As it passes to the data warehouse, the claim information is summarized in several ways—by agent by month, by type of claim by month, etc. At a lower level of detail, the claim is held in the true archival level for an unlimited amount of time. As in the other cases where data passes to the true archival level, only data that has a chance of being needed in the future is kept (which is most of the information found in the operational environment).

These, then, are some examples of granularity and the architected environment as they relate to different industries.

SUMMARY

Choosing the proper levels of granularity for the architected environment is vital to success. The normal way the levels of granularity are chosen is to use common sense, create a small part of the warehouse, and let the user access the data. Then listen very carefully to the user, and take the feedback he/she gives and adjust the levels of granularity appropriately.

The worst stance that can be taken is to try to design all the levels of granularity a priori, then build the data warehouse. Even in the best of circumstances, if 50 percent of the design is done correctly, the design is a good one. The nature of the data warehouse environment is such that the DSS analyst cannot envision what is really needed until he/she sees reports in front of him/her.

5

Data Warehouse and Technology

In many ways, data warehouse requires a simpler set of technological features than its predecessors. There is no online updating with data warehouse; there are only minimal locking needs; only a very basic teleprocessing interface is required, and so forth. Nevertheless, there is a fair number of technological requirements for the data warehouse. This chapter will outline some of those needs.

MANAGING LARGE AMOUNTS OF DATA

The first and easily most important technological requirement for the data warehouse is the ability to manage large amounts of data, as shown in Figure 5.1.

There are many ways that large amounts of data need to be managed—through addressability, through indexing, through extensions of data, through the efficient management of overflow, and so forth. There really are two dimensions to the management of large amounts of data—the capability to manage large amounts at all and the ability to manage large amounts well. Any technology that purports to support the data warehouse must satisfy BOTH the requirements for capability and efficiency.

In the ideal case, the data warehouse developer will build a data

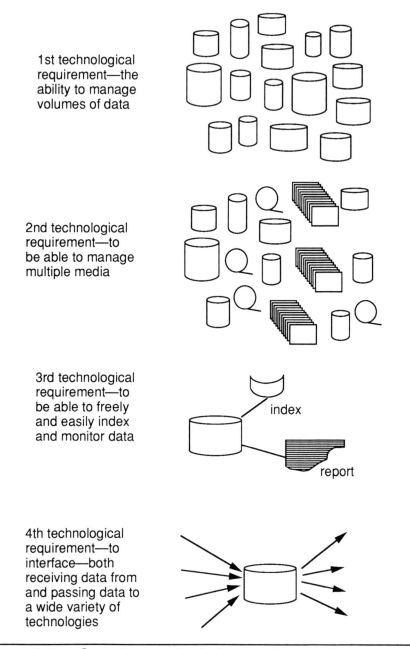

1st technological requirement—the ability to manage volumes of data

2nd technological requirement—to be able to manage multiple media

3rd technological requirement—to be able to freely and easily index and monitor data

index

report

4th technological requirement—to interface—both receiving data from and passing data to a wide variety of technologies

Figure 5.1. Some basic technological requirements for technology supporting a data warehouse.

warehouse assuming that the technology can handle the volumes required. When the designer has to go to extraordinary lengths in design and implementation to map the technology to the data warehouse, then there is a problem with the underlying technology.

Not only is the basic technology and its efficiency an issue insofar as the data warehouse is concerned, but the cost of storage and processing are factors as well.

MANAGING MULTIPLE MEDIA

In conjunction with the requirement of managing large amounts of data efficiently and cost effectively, the technology underlying the data warehouse needs to be able to handle multiple storage media. It is insufficient to manage a mature data warehouse on DASD alone. There is a hierarchy of storage of data—in terms of speed of access and cost of storage. The hierarchy looks like this.

main memory	- very fast	- very expensive
expanded memory	- very fast	- expensive
cache	- very fast	- expensive
DASD	- fast	- moderate
optical disk	- not slow	- not expensive
fiche	- slow	- cheap

The volume of data in the data warehouse and the probability of access are such that a fully populated data warehouse will reside on more than one level of storage. The technology that handles the data warehouse should be able to manage data in multiple storage media.

INDEX/MONITOR DATA

The very essence of the data warehouse is the flexible and unpredictable access of data. This boils down to the ability to access the data quickly and easily. If data in the data warehouse cannot be easily and efficiently indexed, then the data warehouse will not be a success. Of course, there are many design practices that the designer employs to make data as flexible as possible, such as using dual levels of granularity and partitioning data. But the technology must be able to support easy indexing as well. Some of the indexing techniques that often make sense are the support of secondary indexes, the support of sparse indexes, the support of dynamic, temporary indexes, and so forth. Furthermore, the cost of creating the index and using the index cannot be significant.

In the same vein, the data in the data warehouse needs to be able to be monitored at will. The cost of monitoring data cannot be so high and the complexity of monitoring data cannot be so bad that a monitoring program cannot be run whenever necessary.

There are many reasons for monitoring data warehouse data, including the following:

- determining if a reorganization needs to be done
- determining if an index is poorly structured
- determining if much data is in overflow
- determining the statistical composition of the data
- determining available remaining space

If the technology does not support easy and efficient monitoring of data in the warehouse, the technology is not appropriate.

INTERFACES TO MANY TECHNOLOGIES

Another extremely important aspect of the data warehouse is the ability to be able both to receive data from and pass data to a wide variety of technologies. The technology supporting the data warehouse is practically worthless if there are major constraints to the passing of data to/from the data warehouse.

The interface needs to be both efficient and easy to use and able to operate in a batch mode. Operating in an online mode is interesting but not terribly useful.

PROGRAMMER/DESIGNER CONTROL OF DATA PLACEMENT

Because of efficiency of access and update, the programmer/designer needs to have specific control over the placement of data at the physical block/page level, as shown in Figure 5.2.

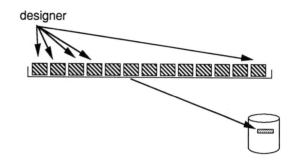

5th technological
requirement—to
allow the designer/
developer to physically
place the data—at the
block/page level—in
an optimal fashion

6th technological
requirement—to
manage data in
parallel

7th technological
requirement—to
have solid metadata
control

8th technological
requirement—to
have a rich language
interface to the
data warehouse

Figure 5.2.   Some more technological requirements for the
            data warehouse.

It is all right for the technology to place the data where it thinks is appropriate, as long as the technology can be explicitly overridden when needed. It is a serious mistake for the technology to insist on the physical placement of data with no overrides from the programmer.

The programmer/designer oftentimes can arrange for the physical placement of data to coincide with the usage of the data. In doing so, there are many economies of access to be gained.

Parallel Storage/Management of Data

One of the most powerful features of data warehouse data management is that of the parallel storage/management of data. When data are stored and managed in a parallel fashion, the gains in performance can be dramatic. As a rule, the performance boost is proportional inversely to the number of physical devices over which the data is scattered, assuming there is an even probability of access for the data.

The entire issue of parallel storage/management of data is too complex and important to be discussed at length here, but it should be mentioned.

Metadata Management

For a variety of reasons, metadata becomes even more important in the data warehouse than in the classical operational environment. Metadata is vital because of the fundamental difference in the development life cycle that is associated with the data warehouse. The data warehouse operates under a heuristic, iterative development life cycle. In order to be effective, the user of the data warehouse must have access to metadata that is accurate and up to date. Without a good source of metadata to operate from, the job of the DSS analyst is much more difficult.

Typically the metadata contains

- data warehouse table structures,
- data warehouse table attribution,
- data warehouse source data (the system of record),
- mapping from the system of record to the data warehouse,

- data model specification,
- extract logging, and
- common routines for access of data.

LANGUAGE INTERFACE

The data warehouse needs to have a rich language specification. Without a robust language, interface entering and accessing data in the warehouse become difficult things to do. In addition, the language accessing data warehouse contents needs to be efficient.

Typically, the language interface to the data warehouse needs to

- be able to access data set at a time,
- be able to access data record at a time,
- specifically ensure that one or more indexes will be used in the satisfaction of a call,
- have an SQL interface, and
- be able to insert data, delete data, or update data.

EFFICIENT LOADING OF DATA

An important technological capability of the data warehouse is to be able to load the data warehouse efficiently, as shown in Figure 5.3.

There are several ways that data is loaded: record at a time through a language interface or en masse with a utility. As a rule, it is much faster to load data efficiently by means of a utility. In addition, there needs to be an efficient loading of the indexes at the same time the data is loaded. In some cases, the loading of the indexes may be deferred in order to spread the workload evenly.

If loading of data warehouse data becomes an insurmountable issue, then the data warehouse becomes unusable.

EFFICIENT INDEX UTILIZATION

Not only must the technology underlying the data warehouse be able to easily support the creation and loading of new indexes, but those indexes that are created must be able to be accessed efficiently.

There are many ways that index access can be made efficient.

9th technological
requirement—to
be able to load
the warehouse
efficiently

10th technological
requirement—to
use indexes
efficiently

11th technological
requirement—to
be able to store
data compactly

12th technological
requirement—to
support compound
keys

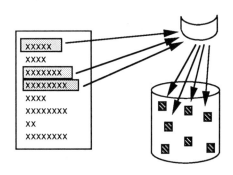

Figure 5.3. Further technological requirements.

- using bit maps
- having multileveled indexes
- storing all or parts of an index in main memory
- compacting the index entries when the order of the data being indexed allows such a compaction
- creating selective indexes and range indexes

There is no end to the ways that an index can be used efficiently.

In addition to the efficient storage and scanning of the index, the subsequent access of data at the primary storage level is important as well. Unfortunately, there are not nearly so many options for optimizing the access of primary data as there are for the access of index data.

COMPACTION OF DATA

The very essence of success in the data warehouse environment is the ability to manage large amounts of data. Central to this goal is the ability to compact data. When data can be compacted it can be stored in a minimal amount of space. This is especially relevant to the data warehouse environment because data in the warehouse environment is seldom updated once inserted into the warehouse. The stability of warehouse data minimizes the problems of space management that arise when tightly compacted data is being updated.

Another advantage of compaction is that the programmer gets the absolute out of a given I/O when data are compactly stored. Of course, there is always the corresponding issue of decompaction of data upon access. While it is true that decompaction requires overhead, the overhead is measured in CPU resources, not I/O resources. As a rule, in the data warehouse environment, I/O resources are much more scarce that CPU resources, so decompaction of data is not a major issue.

COMPOUND KEYS

A simple but important technological requirement of the data warehouse environment is the ability to support compound keys. Compound keys occur everywhere in the data warehouse environment, primarily because of the time variancy of data warehouse data.

VARIABLE-LENGTH DATA

Another simple but very important technological requirement of the data warehouse environment is the ability to manage efficiently variable-length data, as seen in Figure 5.4.

Variable-length data can cause tremendous performance problems when it is constantly being updated and changed. But where variable-length data is stable, as in the case of a data warehouse, there is no inherent performance problem.

On the other hand, the variety of data found in the data warehouse is such that it is mandatory that variable-length structuring of data be supported.

LOCK MANAGEMENT

A standard part of database technology is the lock manager. The lock manager is necessary to ensure that two or more people are not updating the same record at the same time. But update is not done in the data warehouse.

One of the effects of the lock manager is that is consumes a fair amount of resources, even when data are not being updated. Merely turning the lock manager on requires overhead. In order to streamline the data warehouse environment, it is necessary to be able to selectively turn the lock manager off and on.

INDEX-ONLY PROCESSING

A fairly standard database management system feature is that of being able to do index-only processing. On many occasions it is possible to service a request by simply looking in an index (or indexes). When a request can be satisfied by looking only at indexes, it is much more efficient not to have to go to the primary source of data. But not all DBMS are intelligent enough to know that a request can be satisfied in the index.

13th technological requirement—to manage variable-length data efficiently

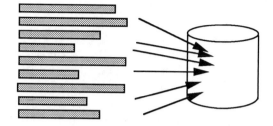

14th technological requirement—to be able to turn on and off the lock manager at will: to be able to explicitly control the lock manager at the programmer level

lock manager

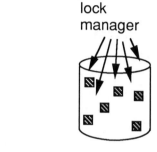

15th technological requirement—to be able to do index-only processing

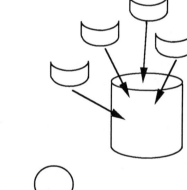

16th technological requirement—to be able to quickly and completely restore data from a bulk medium

Figure 5.4. Technological requirements for the data warehouse.

FAST RESTORE

A simple but important technological feature of the data warehouse environment is the ability to quickly restore a data warehouse table from non-DASD storage quickly. When a restore can be done from secondary storage, there may be enormous savings possible. Without having the ability to quickly restore data from secondary storage, the standard practice is to double the amount of DASD and use one-half of the DASD as a recovery/restore repository.

OTHER TECHNOLOGICAL FEATURES

The features discussed here are only the most important ones. There are many other features that should be considered, but are too numerous or have too little impact to be mentioned here.

It is noteworthy that many other technological features found in classical technology play a small role (if they play a role at all). Some of those features include

- transaction integrity
- high-speed buffering
- row/page level locking
- referential integrity
- VIEWs of data

DUAL LEVELS OF GRANULARITY

One of the interesting aspects of a data warehouse is the dual environments that are often created. One environment is the DASD environment where online/interactive processing is done. The other environment is often a tape handling or mass store environment that has essentially different features. In many cases, the underlying technology that supports the DASD environment is not the same technological environment that supports the mass store environment. Mixing technologies in the data warehouse environment is normal and natural when done this way.

But there is another way that technology can be split that is not normal and natural. It is conceivable that the data warehouse environment—the DASD portion—be split over more than one technology. Unless the split is part of a distributed data warehouse, such a split is not advisable.

SUMMARY

In summary, there are some technological features that are required for satisfactory data warehouse processing. These technological features include a robust language interface, the support of compound keys and variable-length data, and the abilities to

- manage large amounts of data
- manage data on a diverse media
- easily index and monitor data
- interface with a wide number of technologies
- allow the programmer to place the data directly on the physical device
- store and access data in parallel
- have metadata control of the warehouse
- efficiently load the warehouse
- efficiently use indexes
- store data compactly
- selectively turn off the lock manager
- do index only processing
- quickly restore from bulk storage

6

The Distributed Data Warehouse

Most organizations build and maintain a single centralized data warehouse environment. There are many reasons why a single centralized data warehouse environment makes sense.

- The data in the warehouse is integrated across the corporation, and it is only at headquarters that an integrated view is used.
- The volume of data in the data warehouse is such that a single centralized repository of data makes sense.
- Even if data could be integrated, if it were dispersed across multiple local sites, it would be cumbersome to access.

In short, the politics, the economics, and the technology greatly favor a single centralized data warehouse. But there is a need for a distributed data warehouse in a few special cases.

THE DISTRIBUTED DATA WAREHOUSE

To understand when a distributed data warehouse makes sense, consider some basic topologies of processing. Figure 6.1 shows a very common processing topology.

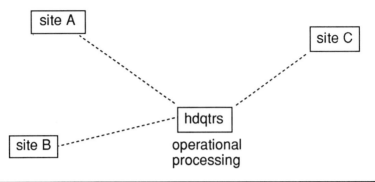

Figure 6.1. A topology of processing representative of many enterprises.

Figure 6.1 shows that an organization has a headquarters and that all processing is done at the headquarters. If there is any processing done whatsoever at the local level, the processing is very, very basic. There might be a series of dumb terminals at the local level. But no significant processing is done locally. In this type of topology it is very unlikely that there will be a need for distributed data warehouse.

One step up the ladder in terms of local processing sophistication is the case where basic capture activity occurs at the local level, as shown in Figure 6.2.

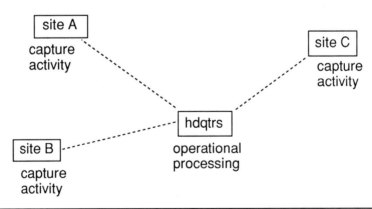

Figure 6.2. In other cases, very basic activity is done at the site level.

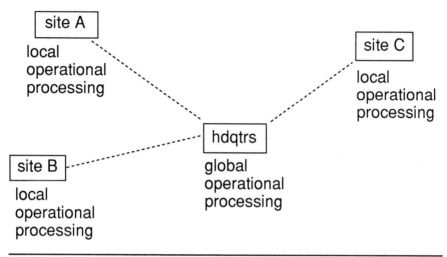

Figure 6.3.   At the other end of the spectrum is the case where much operational processing is done locally.

In Figure 6.2, there is some small amount of processing activity that occurs at the local level. Once the activity is captured, it is shipped to a central location for processing. Under this simple topology it is very unlikely that there will be a need for a distributed data warehouse.

Now, contrast the processing topology shown in Figure 6.3 with the previous two that have been outlined.

In Figure 6.3, there is a fair amount of processing that occurs at the local level. As far as operational processing is concerned, the local sites are autonomous. Only on occasion and for certain types of processing will data and activities be sent to the central organization. It is for this type of organization that some form of distributed data warehouse makes sense.

There are more than one type of distributed data warehouse, as shall be discussed. It is a mistake to think that distributed data warehouse is a binary proposition. Instead, there are degrees of distributed data warehouse.

Most organizations that do not have a great deal of local autonomy and processing have a central data warehouse, as shown in Figure 6.4.

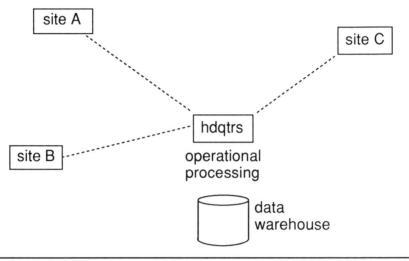

Figure 6.4. Most organizations have a centrally controlled, centrally housed data warehouse.

THE LOCAL DATA WAREHOUSE

There is a form of data warehouse known as a local data warehouse. The local data warehouse contains data that is of interest only to the local level. Figure 6.5 shows a simple example of a series of a local data warehouse.

In Figure 6.5, there is a local data warehouse for different geographical regions or for different technical communities. The local data warehouse serves the same function that any other data warehouse serves, except the scope of the data warehouse is local. In other words, the local data warehouse contains data that is historical in nature and is integrated within the local site.

THE GLOBAL DATA WAREHOUSE

Of course, there can also be a global data warehouse, as shown in Figure 6.6.

The global data warehouse has as its scope the corporation or the enterprise. Each of the local data warehouses has as its scope the local site that it serves. The scope of the global data warehouse

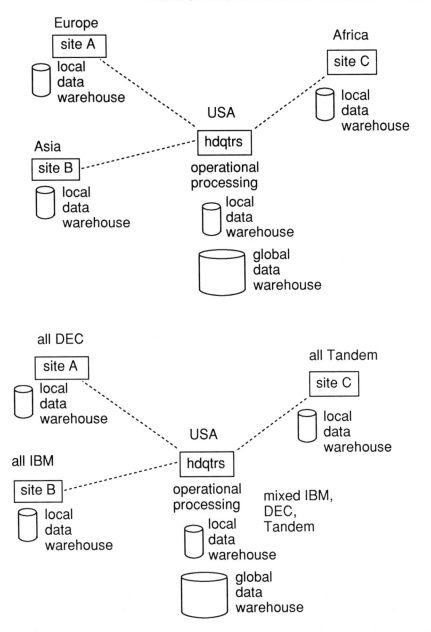

Figure 6.5.   Some circumstances where you might want to create a two-tiered level of data warehouse.

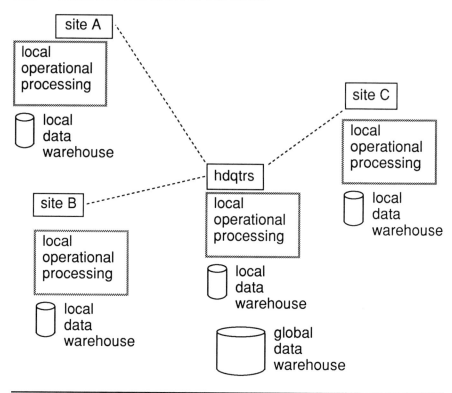

Figure 6.6. What a typical distributed data warehouse might look like.

is corporation. The global data warehouse contains historical data as do the local data warehouses. The source of the data for the local data warehouses is shown in Figure 6.7.

In Figure 6.7, it is seen that each local data warehouse is fed by its own operational systems.

An interesting issue is that of commonality of data among the different local data warehouses. Figure 6.8 shows that each local data warehouse has its own unique structure and content of data.

Any intersection or commonality of data from one local data warehouse to another is purely coincidental. There is no coordination whatsoever of data or processing between the local data warehouses shown in Figure 6.8.

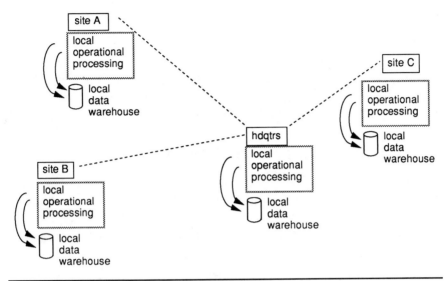

Figure 6.7. The flow of data from the local operational environment to the local data warehouse.

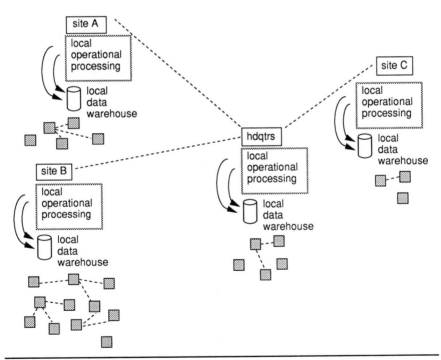

Figure 6.8. The structure and content of the local data warehouses are very different.

But it is reasonable to assume that a corporation will have at least some natural intersections of data from one local site to another. If there is such an intersection, it is best contained in a global data warehouse. Figure 6.9 shows that the global data warehouse is fed from existing local operational systems.

MUTUAL EXCLUSIVITY OF DATA

Not shown, but implicit in Figure 6.9, is the assumption that any data in the local data warehouse are not found in the global data warehouse, and vice versa. For this reason, it is not necessary to feed the global data warehouse from the local data warehouses.

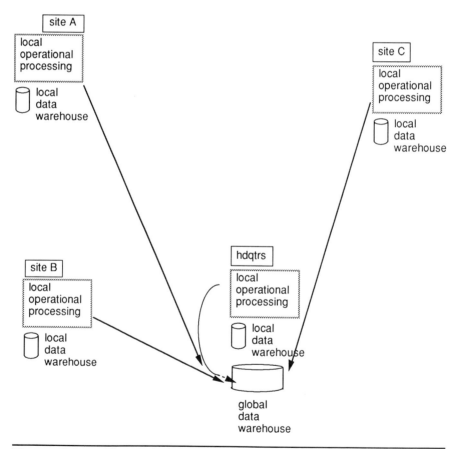

Figure 6.9. The global data warehouse is fed by the outlying operational systems.

The global data warehouse contains data that are common across the corporation and data that are integrated. Central to the success of the distributed data warehouse environment is the mapping of data from the local operational systems to the data structure of the global data warehouse, as seen in Figure 6.10.

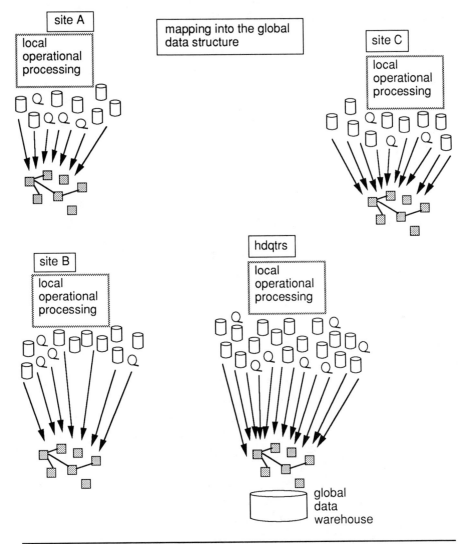

Figure 6.10.   There is a common structure for the global data warehouse. Each local site maps into the common structure differently.

Figure 6.10 shows that there is a common structure of data for the global data warehouse. The common data structure encompasses all common data across the corporation. But there is a different mapping of data from each local site into the global data warehouse. In other words, the global data warehouse is designed and defined centrally, but the mapping of the data from existing local operational systems is a choice made by the local designer and developer.

It is entirely likely that the mapping from local operational systems into global data warehouse systems will not be done as precisely as possible the first time. But over time, as feedback from the user is accumulated, the mapping at the local level improves.

A variation of the data warehouse is that of allowing global data warehouse "staging" areas to be kept at the local level. Figure 6.11 illustrates this option.

Figure 6.11 shows that each local area stages global warehouse data before passing the data to the central location. In many circumstances, this approach may be technologically mandatory. There is an important issue associated with this approach—should the locally staged global data warehouse be emptied after it is transferred to the global level? If the data are not deleted locally, then there will be redundant data. However, under certain conditions, some amount of redundancy may be called for. This issue must be decided and policies and procedures put into place.

REDUNDANCY

In conjunction with the issue of redundancy of data arises the issue of redundancy between local data warehouses and global data warehouses, as seen in Figure 6.12.

Figure 6.12 shows that, as a policy, there is no redundant data between the local levels and the global levels of data (and in this regard, it matters not whether global data is stored locally in a staging area or centrally). The minute there exists redundant data between the local data warehouse and the global data warehouse, it is an indication that the scope of the different warehouses has not been defined properly. And when there is a difference of opinion between the local and global scopes, it is only a matter of time before "spider web" systems start to appear. For this reason, it should be a matter of policy that global data and local data be mutually exclusive.

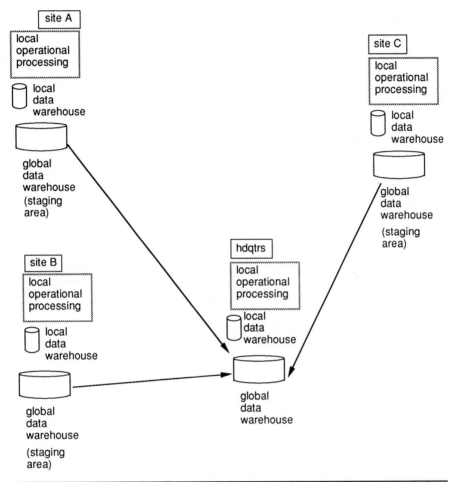

Figure 6.11.   There is the possibility of staging the global
data warehouse at the local level, then
passing it to the global data warehouse at the
headquarters level.

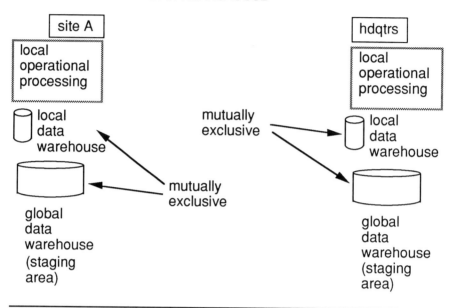

Figure 6.12.   Data can exist in either the local data warehouse or the global data warehouse, but not both.

ACCESS OF GLOBAL DATA

In line with policies required to manage the different data warehouses, there is the issue of access of data. At first, this issue seems to be almost trivial. But there are some important ramifications. Figure 6.13 illustrates some of the aspects of the issue of access of data.

Figure 6.13 shows that some local sites are accessing global data. Depending upon what is being asked for, this may or may not be an appropriate usage of data warehouse data. If the global data is being used informationally and on a one-time only basis, then its access at the local level is probably all right.

As a principle, local data should be used locally and global data should be used globally. The question must be raised, why is global analysis being done locally? As a rule, there is no good reason for it.

Another issue is that of the routing of requests for information into the architected information environment. When there was only a single central data warehouse, there was little issue over

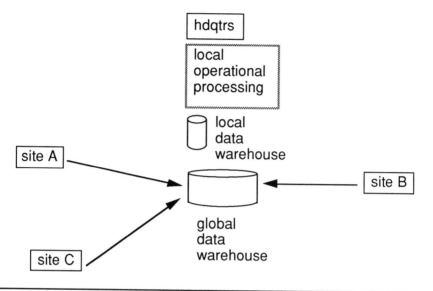

Figure 6.13. An important issue that needs resolution is whether local sites should be accessing the global data warehouse.

where a request for information was routed. But when data are distributed over a complex landscape, such as a distributed data warehouse landscape, as shown in Figure 6.14, then there is some amount of work required to make sure the request is being addressed at the appropriate place.

For example, asking a local site to determine what total corporate salaries are is an incorrect thing to do. By the same token, asking the central data warehouse group what a contractor was paid last month at a particular site for a particular service is likewise an inappropriate thing to do.

A related yet separate issue not addressed in this chapter is that of global operational data. This chapter has taken the stance that every local site will have its own unique data and processing. But it is entirely possible that there will be a degree of commonality between the operational systems found at each local site.

Underlying the whole issue of distributed data warehouse is the issue of complexity. In a simple central data warehouse environment, roles and responsibilities are fairly straightforward. But in a

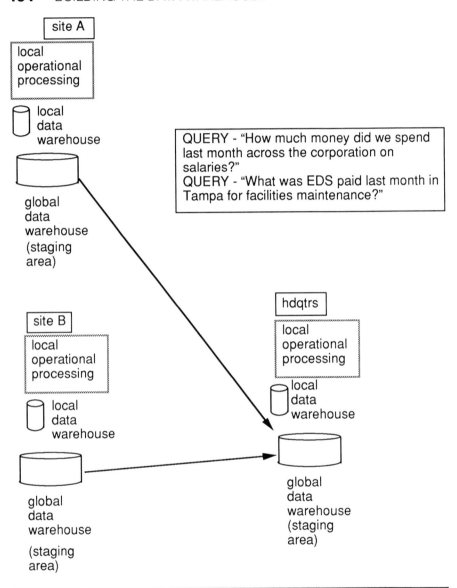

site A

local
operational
processing

local
data
warehouse

global
data
warehouse
(staging
area)

QUERY - "How much money did we spend
last month across the corporation on
salaries?"
QUERY - "What was EDS paid last month in
Tampa for facilities maintenance?"

hdqtrs

local
operational
processing

local
data
warehouse

site B

local
operational
processing

local
data
warehouse

global
data
warehouse
(staging
area)

global
data
warehouse
(staging
area)

Figure 6.14. Queries need to be routed to different parts of
the architecture to be answered properly.

distributed data warehouse environment, the issues of scope, coordination, metadata, responsibilities, transfer of data, local mapping, etc., make the environment complex indeed.

SUMMARY

Most environments operate from a single centralized data warehouse. But in some circumstances there can be a distributed data warehouse. There may be local data warehouses that house data unique to and of interest to the local operating site. There may also be a globally distributed data warehouse. The structure and content of the distributed global data warehouse are decided centrally. The mapping of data into the global data warehouse is decided locally.

The coordination and administration of the distributed data warehouse environment is much more complex than that of the single-site data warehouse.

7

EIS and Data Warehouse

EIS—executive information systems—is one of the most potent forms of computing. Through EIS the executive analyst can pinpoint problems and detect trends that are of vital importance to management. In a sense, EIS represents the most sophisticated usage of the computer.

EIS processing is the processing that is tailored for the executive in order to make decisions. EIS processing looks across broad vistas and picks out the aspects that are relevant to the running of the business. Some of the typical uses of EIS are

- trend analysis and detection,
- key ratio indicator measurement and tracking,
- problem monitoring, and
- competitive analysis.

A SIMPLE EXAMPLE

As a simple example of how EIS analysis might appear to an executive, consider Figure 7.1.

Figure 7.1 shows information on insurance policies offered by an insurance company. Quarter by quarter, the new life, health, and

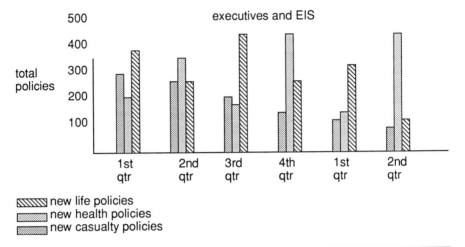

Figure 7.1. A chart typical of EIS processing.

casualty policy sales are tracked. The simple graph shown in Figure 7.1 is a good starting point for an executive's probing into the state of the business.

Once the executive has seen the overall information, he/she can probe more deeply, as shown by the trend analysis in Figure 7.2.

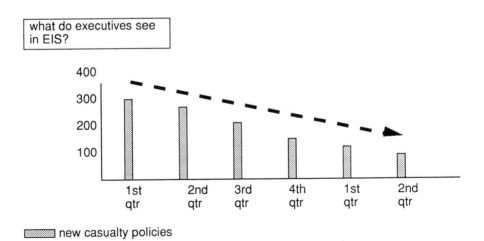

Figure 7.2. Trends—new casualty policy sales are slacking off.

In Figure 7.2, the executive has isolated new casualty sales from new life sales and new health sales. Looking just at new casualty sales, the executive identifies a trend. Each quarter new casualty sales are dropping off. Having identified the trend, the executive can further investigate why sales are dropping.

The EIS analysis alerts the executive as to what the trends are. It is then up to the executive to discover the underlying reasons for the trends.

The executive is interested in both negative and positive trends. If business is getting worse, why? And at what rate? What can be done to remedy the situation? Or, if business is picking up, why? What factors are responsible for the upturn? What can be done to accelerate the success factors? Can the success factors be applied in other parts of the business?

But trends are not the only type of analysis that is accommodated by EIS. Another type of useful analysis is that of comparisons. Figure 7.3 shows a comparison that might be found in an EIS analysis.

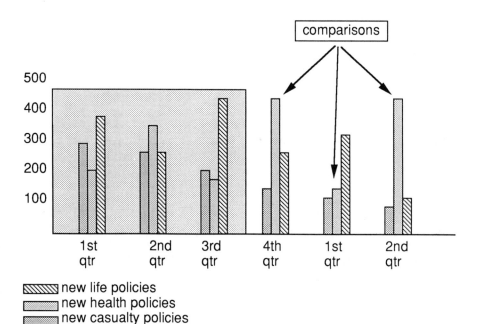

Figure 7.3. Why is there the extreme difference in sales of new health policies for the past three quarters?

Looking at fourth quarter data, first quarter data, and second quarter data in Figure 7.3, the question can be asked, Why is there such a difference in sales of new health policies for the past three quarters? The EIS processing alerts the manager to these differences. It is then the job of the EIS analyst to determine the underlying reasons.

For the manager of a large, diverse enterprise, EIS allows a look at the activities of the enterprise in many ways. Trying to keep track of a large number of activities is much more difficult than trying to keep track of just a few activities. In that sense, EIS can be used to expand the scope of control of a manager.

But trend analysis and comparisons are not the only means the manager has to use EIS effectively. Another approach is the "slice and dice approach." Here the analyst takes basic information and groups it one way and analyzes it, then groups it another way and reanalyzes it. Slicing and dicing allows the manager to have many different perspectives of the activities that are occurring.

DRILL-DOWN ANALYSIS

In order to do slicing and dicing, it is necessary to be able to "drill down" data. Drilling down data refers to the ability to start at a summary number and to break that summary into a successively finer set of summarizations. By being able to get at the detail beneath a summary number, the manager can get a feel for what is happening, especially where the summary number is surprising. Figure 7.4 shows a simple example of drill-down analysis.

In Figure 7.4, the manager has seen second quarter summary results and wants to explore them further. The manager then looks at the regions that have contributed to the summary analysis. The regions' figures that are analyzed are the Western region, the Southeast region, the Northeast region, and the Central region. In looking at the numbers of each region, the manger decides to look more closely at the Northeast region's numbers.

The Northeast's numbers are made up of totals from New York, Massachusetts, Connecticut, Pennsylvania, New Jersey, Virginia, Maine, Rhode Island, and Vermont. Of these states, the manager then decides to look more closely at the numbers for New York state. The different cities in New York state that have outlets are then queried.

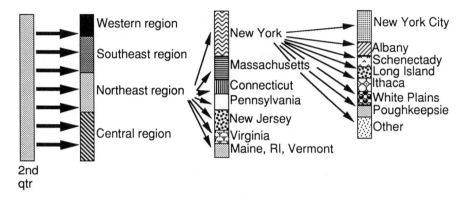

Figure 7.4. In order to make sense of the numbers shown by an EIS, the numbers need to support a "drill-down" process.

In each case, the manager has selected a path of going from summary to detail, then to a successively lower level. In such a fashion, the manager can determine where the results that are troublesome are. Once having identified the anomalies, the manager then knows where to look for a closer explanation.

There is plenty of very sophisticated software that can be used in EIS to present the results to a manager. The difficult part of EIS is not in the graphical presentation but in discovering and preparing the numbers that go into the graphics, as seen in Figure 7.5.

EIS is perfectly capable of supporting the drill-down process from the graphical perspective as long as the data exists in the first place. But if the data to analyze does not exist, the drill-down process becomes very tedious and awkward, certainly not something the executive wants to do.

SUPPORTING THE DRILL-DOWN PROCESS

Creating the basis of data on which to do drill-down analysis, then, is the major obstacle to successfully implementing the drill-down process, as seen in Figure 7.6.

Indeed, some studies indicate that $9 is spent on drill-down data preparation for every $1 spent on EIS software and hardware.

Exaggerating the problem is the fact that the executive is

Figure 7.5. EIS software supports the drill-down process *as long as the data that is needed is available and is structured properly.*

Figure 7.6. Creating the base of data on which to do EIS processing is the hard part.

constantly changing his/her mind about what is of interest. Figure 7.7 shows the constantly changing nature of what interests the executive.

On day one, the executive is interested in the corporation's financial activities. The EIS analyst spends a large effort in developing the

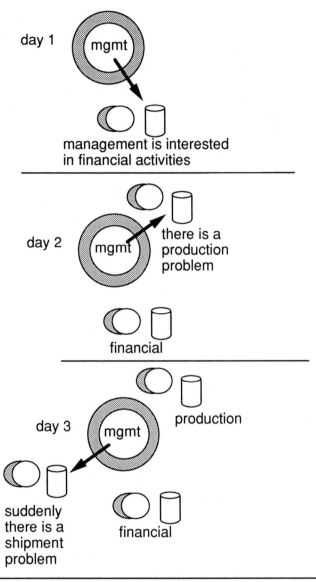

day 1

mgmt

management is interested
in financial activities

day 2

mgmt

there is a
production
problem

financial

day 3

mgmt

production

suddenly
there is a
shipment
problem

financial

Figure 7.7.　•　management's attention is constantly
shifting
•　the shift is in a random pattern
•　management always wants the information
NOW!
•　at the end of the data, management wants
the data integrated as well

underlying data to support EIS interest. Then on day two, there is unexpectedly a production problem and management's attention is turned there. The EIS analyst scurries around and tries to gather the data needed by the executive. On day three, the EIS analyst is directed to the problems that have developed in shipping.

Management's focus shifts with every new problem or opportunity that arises. There simply is no predictable pattern to what management will be interested in tomorrow. In turn, the EIS analyst is at the end of a whip—the wrong end! The EIS analyst is forever in a reactive state. Furthermore, given the work that is required of the EIS analyst in order to build the base of data needed for EIS analysis, the EIS analyst is constantly behind.

THE DATA WAREHOUSE

It is into this environment that the data warehouse operates. The data warehouse is tailormade for the needs of the EIS analyst. When the data warehouse has been built, the job of the EIS is infinitely easier than when there is no foundation of data on which to function. Figure 7.8 shows how the data warehouse supports the need for EIS data.

With a data warehouse, the EIS analyst

- does not have to search for the definitive source of data,
- does not have to create special extract programs from existing systems,
- does not have to worry about unintegrated data,
- does not have to worry about detailed and summary data and the linkage between the two,
- does not have to worry about finding an appropriate time basis of data, and
- does not have to worry about management constantly or changing its mind about what needs to be looked at next.

In short, the data warehouse provides the basis of data that the EIS analyst needs to effectively support EIS processing. With a fully populated data warehouse in place, the analyst can be in a proactive stance—not an eternally reactive stance—with regards to answering management's needs. The EIS analyst's job changes

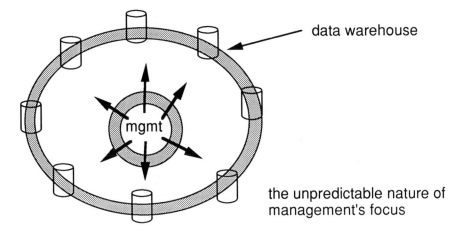

data warehouse

mgmt

the unpredictable nature of
management's focus

Figure 7.8. The data warehouse

- is in place when needed,
- is integrated,
- has detailed and summary data,
- covers all the wide topics needed by
  management, and
- has the lengthy time basis of data needed
  for trending.

from that of data engineer to that of doing true analysis on data in
the face of a data warehouse.

WHERE TO TURN

The EIS analyst can turn to different places in the architecture in
order to get data, as shown in Figure 7.9.

In Figure 7.9, it is seen that the EIS analyst can go to the
individual level of processing, the departmental level of processing,
the lightly summarized level of processing, or the true archival
level in order to get data. There is no rule that says the EIS analyst
must get data from anywhere.

In addition, there is a normal sequence or hierarchy in which the
EIS analyst goes after data to serve management's needs. The
order is indicated in Figure 7.9.

Figure 7.9. Another perspective of where EIS turns to to get data.

There is a very good reason for the order shown, as indicated in Figure 7.10.

By going from the individual level of processing to the true archival level of processing, the analyst by de facto does drill-down analysis. The most summarized data found in the architected environment is found at the individual level. The supporting level of summary for the individual level is the departmental level. Supporting the summaries found at the departmental level is data found at the data warehouse lightly summarized level. And finally, the light summarization found at the data warehouse level is supported by true archival data. The sequence of summaries just described is precisely what is required to support drill-down EIS analysis.

Almost by default, the data warehouse lays a path for drill-down analysis. At the different levels of the data warehouse, and

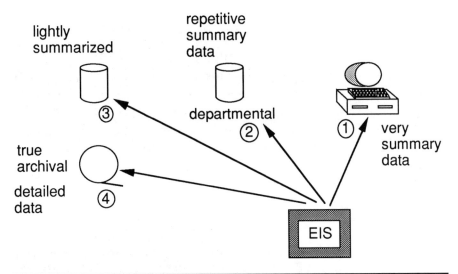

Figure 7.10. Another perspective is that in going from individual levels of processing to true archival data, the drill-down process is accommodated.

throughout the summarization process, data is related by means of a key structure. The key structure itself, or the derivations of the key structure, allow the data to be related so that drill-down analysis is an easy thing to do.

EVENT MAPPING

A useful technique in using the data warehouse for EIS processing is that of event mapping. The simplest way to depict event mapping is to start with a simple trend line, as shown by Figure 7.11.

Figure 7.11 shows that corporate revenues have varied by month, as expected. The trend has been calculated from data found in the data warehouse. The trend of revenues in and of itself is interesting but gives only a superficial view of what is going on with the corporation. To enhance the view, events are mapped onto the trend line, as shown in Figure 7.12.

In Figure 7.12, three notable events have been mapped to the corporate revenue trend line—the introduction of a "spring colors"

Figure 7.11. Simple trends.

Figure 7.12. Mapping events against a trend line.

line of products, the advent of a salesmen's incentive program, and the introduction of competition. Now the relationship between corporate revenue and significant events begins to take on a different perspective. Looking at the diagram in Figure 7.12, the conclusion can be drawn that the introduction of a new line of products and a new incentive plan have boosted revenue and that competition is starting to have an effect in the latter part of the year.

For some sorts of events, event mapping is the only way to measure the results. Some events and activities cannot be measured directly and have to be measured in a correlative fashion. Cost justification and actual cost benefit cannot be measured any other way for some types of events.

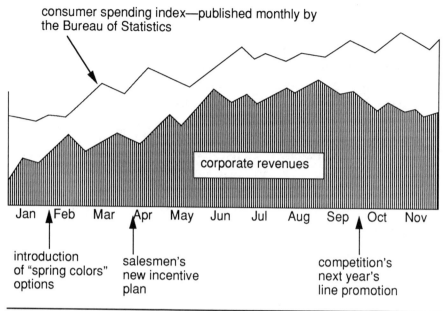

consumer spending index—published monthly by
the Bureau of Statistics

corporate revenues

Jan   Feb   Mar   Apr   May   Jun   Jul   Aug   Sep   Oct   Nov

introduction
of "spring colors"
options

salesmen's
new incentive
plan

competition's
next year's
line promotion

Figure 7.13.   Superimposing another trend analysis over the
existing one to gain another perspective.

However, misleading conclusions can be drawn by looking at
correlative information. It often helps to look at more than one set
of trends that relate to the events at hand. As an example of looking
at multiple trends, Figure 7.13 shows that corporate revenues are
matched against consumer confidence index to produce a diagram
packed with even more perspective.

Looking at Figure 7.13, the executive can make up his/her own
mind whether events that have been mapped have shaped sales or
not.

The data warehouse can store both the internally generated
revenue numbers and the externally generated consumer confidence numbers.

SUMMARY

There is a very strong affinity between the needs of the EIS analyst
and the data warehouse. The data warehouse explicitly supports
ALL of the EIS analyst's needs. With a data warehouse in place, the

EIS analyst can be in a proactive position rather than a reactive position.

The needs of the EIS analyst that are supported by the data warehouse include

- the need of management for very quick information,
- the need of management to change their mind,
- the need of management to look at integrated data,
- the need of management to look at data over a spectrum of time, and
- the need of management to be able to drill down.

8

External/Unstructured Data and the Data Warehouse

Most organizations build their first data warehouse efforts on the data whose source is existing systems. In almost every case, the data that comes from existing systems can be termed internal, structured data. The data comes from the internals of the corporation and the data has been already shaped into a regularly occurring format.

But there is a whole host of other data that legitimately has use to a corporation that is not generated from the corporation's own systems. This class of data is called external data and usually enters the corporation in an unstructured, unpredictable format. Figure 8.1 shows external data and unstructured data entering the data warehouse.

The data warehouse is the ideal place to store external and unstructured data. If external and unstructured data is not stored in a centrally located place, there are several problems that are sure to arise, as seen in Figure 8.2.

Figure 8.2 shows that when external and unstructured data enters the corporation in an undisciplined fashion,

- the identity of the source of the data is lost, and
- there is no coordination whatsoever in the orderly use of the data.

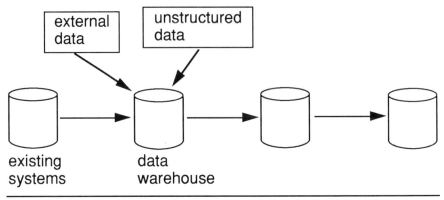

Figure 8.1. External and unstructured data both belong in the data warehouse.

Typically, when external data is not entered into the data warehouse, it comes into the corporation by means of the PC. There is nothing wrong with entering data at the PC level, per se. But almost always when data is entered at the PC level it is entered manually through a spreadsheet, and there is absolutely no attempt to capture information about the source of data as well as the data. For example, in Figure 8.2 an analyst sees a report in the *Wall Street Journal*. The next day, the analyst uses the data from the *Wall Street Journal* as part of a report. The original source of the data is lost as it is entered into the corporate mainstream of data.

Another difficulty with the laissez faire approach to external data is that at a later point in time it is hard to recall the data. The data is entered into the corporation's systems, it is used once, and then it disappears. At a later point in time (even a few weeks later), it is hard to reaccess the data for further use, and this is unfortunate, because much of the data coming from external sources is quite useful over the spectrum of time.

The types of data that come from external sources are many and diverse. Some of the typical sources of interesting data include the following:

- the *Wall Street Journal*
- *Business Week*
- *Forbes*

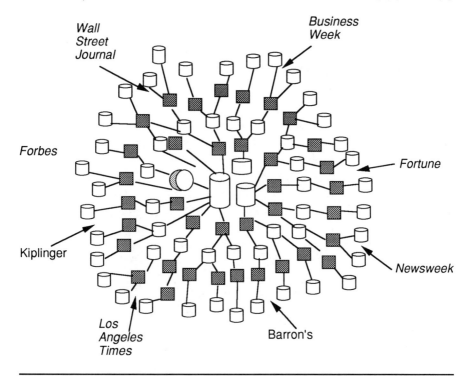

Figure 8.2. The problem with external and unstructured data is

- its source is stripped upon entering the corporation, and
- one analyst is not aware that another analyst has brought in similar information.

- *Fortune*
- industry newsletters
- technology reports
- Dun and Bradstreet
- reports generated by consultants specifically for the corporation
- Equifax reports
- competitive analysis reports
- marketing comparison and analysis reports
- sales analysis and comparison reports
- new product announcements

In addition, there are several reports internal to the corporation that are of interest as well.

- the auditor's quarterly report
- the annual report

There are several issues that relate to the use and storage of external and unstructured data in the data warehouse. Figure 8.3 shows some of those issues.

In Figure 8.3, one problem of unstructured data is that of frequency of availability. Unlike internally appearing data, there is no real pattern of appearance of external data. The frequency of appearance is a problem in that constant monitoring must be set up to ensure that the right data is captured.

The second problem with external data is that of the form of the data. The form of the external data is totally undisciplined. In order to be useful, and in order for the data to be placed in the warehouse, a certain amount of reformatting of data must be accomplished to transform external data into an internally acceptable and usable form.

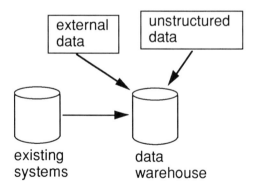

Figure 8.3.   Other issues:

- the frequency of entry
- the form of data
- the unpredictability

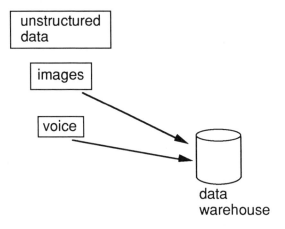

Figure 8.4.   Some forms of unstructured data that can be
stored in the data warehouse.

The third factor that makes external data hard to capture is its unpredictability. External data may come from practically any source at almost any time. The unpredictable nature of the availability of external data makes it very difficult for it to be consistently and completely captured.

In addition to external data that might come out of a magazine article or a consultant's report, there is another whole class of data that is just now able to be automated—unstructured data, shown in Figure 8.4.

The two most common types of unstructured data are in the forms of images and voice. Image data is data stored as pictures. Voice data is data stored digitally and able to be translated back into a voice format. The issues of image data and voice data stem primarily from technology. The technology to capture and manipulate image and voice data is not nearly as mature as more conventional technology. In addition, even when image and voice data can be captured, their storage requires huge amounts of DASD, and their recall and display or playback can be awkward and slow.

Nevertheless, there are many possibilities in the capturing of unstructured information and the storage in a data warehouse.

METADATA AND EXTERNAL DATA

Metadata is an important component of the data warehouse in any scenario. But metadata takes on an entirely different dimension in the face of storing and managing external and unstructured data. Figure 8.5 shows the role of metadata.

Metadata is important because it is through metadata that external data is registered, accessed, and controlled in the data warehouse environment. The best explanation of the importance of metadata is witnessed by the typical contents of metadata in the data warehouse for external data, such as the following:

- document ID
- date of entry into the warehouse
- description of the document
- source of the document
- date of source of the document
- classification of the document

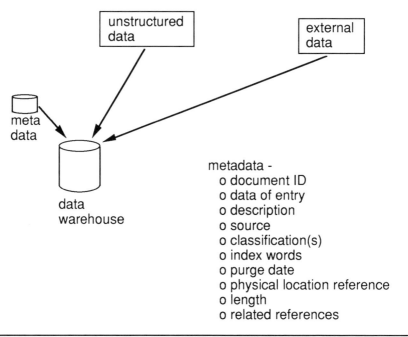

Figure 8.5. Metadata takes on a new role in the face of external and unstructured data.

- index words
- purge date
- physical location reference
- length of the document
- related references

It is through the metadata that a manager determines much information about the external data. In many instances, the manager will look at the metadata without ever looking at the source document. Scanning metadata eliminates much work for the manager in ruling out documents that are not relevant or are out of date.

Properly built and maintained metadata, then, is absolutely essential to the operation of the data warehouse insofar as external data is concerned.

In association with metadata is another type of data—notification data. Figure 8.6 shows notification data.

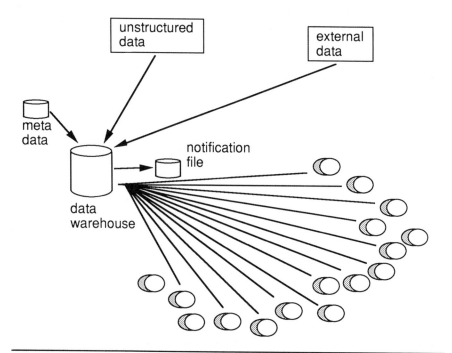

Figure 8.6.   Another nice feature of external data and metadata is the ability to create a tailored notification file.

Notification data is merely a file created for the users of the system that indicates classifications of data interesting to the user. When data is entered into the data warehouse and into the metadata, a check is made to see who is interested in the data. Upon discovering that someone is interested in the data that has just been captured, a notification is made to the person so that the person will know that external data of interest has been captured.

STORING EXTERNAL/UNSTRUCTURED DATA

External data and unstructured data can actually be stored in the data warehouse if it is convenient and cost effective to do so. But in many cases it will not be possible or economical to store all external data in the data warehouse. Instead, an entry is made in the metadata of the warehouse describing where the actual body of external data can be found, and the external data is stored elsewhere, where it is convenient, as shown in Figure 8.7.

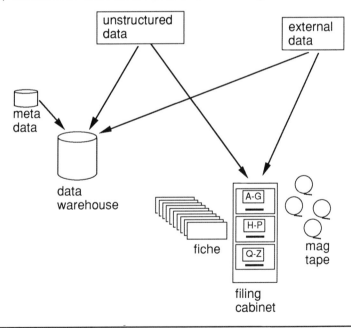

Figure 8.7. In every case, external data/unstructured data is registered with the metadata, but the actual data may or may not be stored in the data warehouse based on the size of the data and the probability of access.

In Figure 8.7, it is seen that external data may be stored in a filing cabinet, on fiche, on magnetic tape, etc. Of course, external data can be stored in the data warehouse if desired.

MODELLING AND EXTERNAL/ UNSTRUCTURED DATA

What is the role of the data model and external data? Figure 8.8 reflects the dilemma.

The normal role of the data model is the shaping of the environment, usually in terms of design. But external data and unstructured data are not malleable to any extent at all. Therefore it appears that there is very little relationship between the data

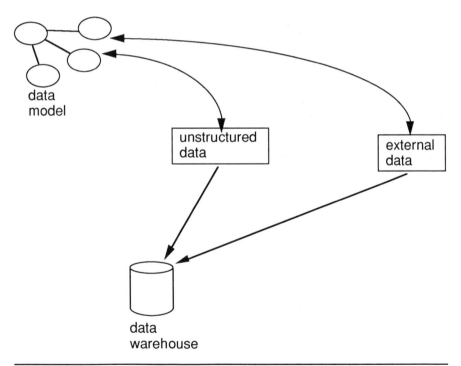

Figure 8.8.   There usually is only a faint resemblance of external data/unstructured data to the data model. Furthermore, there is nothing that can be done about reshaping external data and unstructured data.

model and external data. About the best that can be done is to note the differences between the data model and the interpretation of key phrases and words from that used inside the external data. Attempting to use the data model for any serious reshaping of the data is a mistake.

SECONDARY REPORTS

Not only can primary data be put in the data warehouse, but when data is repetitive in nature, secondary reports can be created from the detailed data over time. For example, take the month-end Dow Jones average report, shown in Figure 8.9.

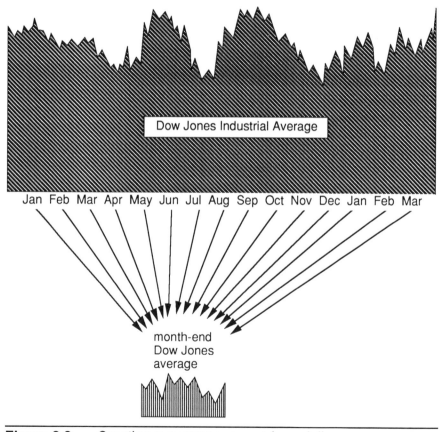

Figure 8.9. Creating a summary report from daily or monthly recurring information.

In Figure 8.9, Dow Jones information comes into the data warehouse environment daily. The daily information is useful, but of even more interest are the long-term trends that are formed. At the end of the month, the Dow Jones average is shuffled off into a "secondary" report. The secondary report then becomes part of the store of external data contained in the data warehouse.

ARCHIVING DATA

Every piece of information—external or otherwise—has a useful lifetime. Once past that lifetime, it is not economical to keep the information. An essential part of managing external data is in deciding what the useful lifetime of the data is. Even after this is determined, there still remains an issue as to whether the data should be discarded or put into archives. As a rule, external data may be removed from the data warehouse and placed on less expensive storage. The metadata reference to the external data is updated to reflect the new storage place and is left in the metadata store. The cost of an entry into the metadata store is so low that once put there, it is best left there.

SUMMARY

In summary, the data warehouse is capable of holding much more than internal, structured data. There is much information relevant to the running of the company that comes from sources outside the company.

External data is captured, and information about the metadata is stored in the data warehouse metadata. The metadata serves as an executive index to information. In addition, a "notification" service is often provided whenever a new entry is made into the data warehouse.

External and unstructured data may or may not actually be stored in the data warehouse.

9

Migration to the Architected Environment

Any architecture that must be implemented all at once, in a big bang, is doomed to failure in today's world. There simply is too much risk, too long a period to wait until there is a payback, and the unreality of trying to freeze changes to consider any path that is revolutionary, rather than revolutionary.

It is very good news indeed that migrating to the architected data warehouse environment is a step-by-step activity that is accomplished one finite deliverable at a time. The most successful implementations of the architected environment have been those where the data warehouse has been built one iteration at a time. In doing so, the data warehouse can be built for a minimum of manpower resources and can be built with absolutely minimal disruption to the existing applications environment.

In this chapter, a generic migration plan and a methodology for development will be discussed. The methodology is described in detail in the appendix. The migration plan has been successfully followed by a wide number of companies. It is anything but a fanciful flight. The methodology has been gleaned from the experiences of a number of companies. Of course, each company will have its own diversions and permutations. But the migration plan and methodology have met with enough success in enough diverse companies to merit the confidence of the general-purpose developer.

A MIGRATION PLAN

The beginning point for the migration plan is a data model. The data model represents the information needs of the corporation. It represents what the corporation needs, not what the corporation currently has. It is built with no consideration of technology.

The data model may be built internally or may have been generated from a generic data model. The data model needs to identify (at a minimum!) the following:

- the major subjects of the corporation
- the relationships between the major subjects
- the groupings of keys and attributes that more fully represent the major subjects, including
  - the attributes of the major subjects,
  - the keys of the major subjects,
  - the repeating groups of keys and attributes,
  - connectors between major subject areas, and
  - subtyping relationships.

In theory, it is possible to build the architected environment without a data model. However, in practice it is never done. Trying to build an architected environment without a data model is like trying to navigate without a map. It can be done, but it is very prone to trial and error. It is like a person who has never been outside of Texas landing at New York's La Guardia airport and driving to midtown Manhattan with no map and no instructions. It can be done (perhaps!), but all sensibilities suggest that a map is a superior way to go.

Figure 9.1 shows that building or otherwise acquiring a data model is the starting point for the migration process.

After the data model is in place, the next activity is the definition of the system of record. The system of record is defined in terms of the existing systems the corporation already has. Usually these systems are affectionately known as the "mess."

The system of record is nothing more than the identification of

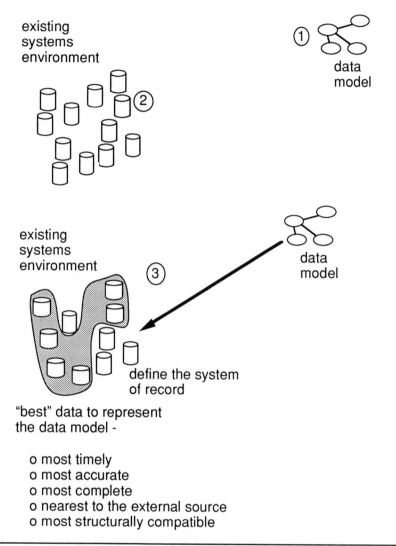

existing
systems
environment

data
model

existing
systems
environment

data
model

define the system
of record

"best" data to represent
the data model -

o most timely
o most accurate
o most complete
o nearest to the external source
o most structurally compatible

Figure 9.1.   Migration to the architected environment.

the "best" data the corporation has. The data model is used as a benchmark for determining what the best data are. In other words, the data architect starts with the data model and asks what data do we have in hand that best fulfill the data identified in the data model. It is understood that the fit will be less than a perfect one. In some cases there will be no data in the existing systems environment that exemplifies the data in the data model. In other cases there will be many sources of data in the existing systems environment that contribute data to the systems of record, each under different circumstances.

The "best" source of existing data is determined by the following criteria:

- What data in the existing systems environment is the most complete?
- What data in the existing systems environment is the most timely?
- What data in the existing systems environment is the most accurate?
- What data in the existing systems environment is the closest to the source of entry into the existing systems environment?
- What data in the existing systems environment conforms the most closely to the structure of the data model? In terms of keys? In terms of attributes? In terms of grouping of data attributes together?

Using the data model and the criteria described above, the analyst defines the system of record.

After the system of record is defined, the next step is to design the data warehouse, as shown in Figure 9.2.

If the data modelling activity has been done properly, the design of the data warehouse is a simple activity. Only a few aspects of the data model need to be changed to turn the data model into a data warehouse design. Principally, the following needs to be done:

- An element of timeliness needs to be added to the key structure.
- All purely operational data needs to be eliminated.
- Referential integrity relationships need to be turned into "artifacts."
- Derived data that is constantly being calculated needs to be added to the design.
- The structure of the data needs to altered when appropriate for
  - adding arrays of data,
  - adding data redundantly,

existing
systems
environment

design the data
warehouse

existing
systems
environment

design the data
warehouse

extract
integrate
change time basis of data
condense data
efficiently scan data

Figure 9.2.   Migration to the architected environment.

- further separating data under the right conditions, and
- merging tables when appropriate.

The data warehouse, once designed, is organized by subject area. Typical subject areas are

- customer
- product
- sale
- account
- activity
- shipment

Within the subject area there will be many separate tables, each of which is connected by a common key.

After the data warehouse is designed, the next step is to design and build the interfaces between the system of record—in the operational environment—and the data warehouses. The interfaces populate the data warehouse on a regular basis.

At first glance, the interfaces appear to be merely an extract process, and it is true that extract processing does occur. But there are many more activities that occur at the point of interface as well.

- integration of data from the operational, application oriented environment
- the alteration of the time basis of data
- the condensation of data
- the efficient scanning of the existing systems environment

Most of these issues have been discussed elsewhere in this book.

It is of interest that the vast majority of resources required to build a data warehouse occur at this point. It is not unusual for 80 percent of the manpower required to build a data warehouse to be consumed here. In laying out the development activities for the building of a data warehouse, most developers overestimate the time required for other activities and underestimate the time required for designing and building the operational to data warehouse interface.

Once the interface programs are designed and built, the next activity is to start the population of the first subject area, as shown in Figure 9.3.

There are many good reasons to populate only a fraction of the data needed in a data warehouse at this point. It is very likely that changes to the data will need to be made. Populating only a small amount of data means that those changes can be made easily and quickly. Populating a large amount of data greatly diminishes the flexibility of the data in the data warehouse. Once the end user has had a chance to look at the data and give feedback to the data architect, then it is safe to populate large volumes of data.

The population process continues for a long period (really, indefinitely!). In addition, the data in the warehouse continues to be changed.

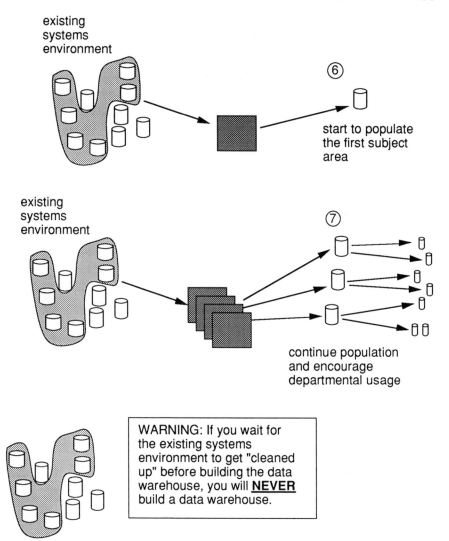

Figure 9.3. Migration to the architected environment.

There must be a word of caution at this point: IF YOU WAIT FOR EXISTING SYSTEMS TO BE CLEANED UP, YOU WILL NEVER BUILD A DATA WAREHOUSE. The issues and activities of the existing systems operational environment must be independent of the issues and activities of the data warehouse environment.

One observation that is worthwhile at this point is the frequency of refreshment of data warehouse data. As a rule, data warehouse data should be refreshed no more frequently than every 24 hours. By making sure that there is at least a 24-hour time delay in the loading of data, the data warehouse developer minimizes the temptation to try to turn the data warehouse into an operational environment. The data warehouse serves the DSS needs of the company, not the operational needs. Most operational processing depends on data being accurate as of the moment of access (i.e., current value data). By insuring that there is a 24-hour delay (at the least), the data warehouse developer adds an important ingredient that maximizes the chances for success.

THE FEEDBACK LOOP

At the heart of success in the development of the data warehouse is the feedback loop between the data architect and the DSS analyst, shown in Figure 9.4.

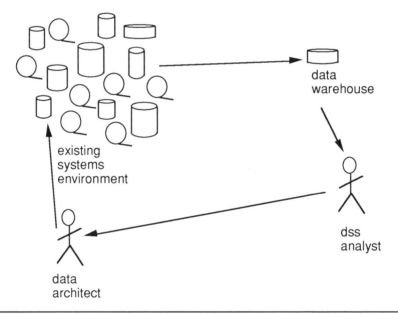

Figure 9.4.   The crucial feedback loop between DSS analyst and data architect.

Figure 9.4 shows that the data warehouse is populated from existing systems. The DSS analyst uses the data warehouse as a basis for analysis. Upon finding new opportunities, the DSS analyst conveys those requirements back to the data architect, who makes the appropriate adjustments.

There are a few observations about this feedback loop that are of vital importance to the success of the data warehouse environment.

- The DSS analyst operates—quite legitimately—in a "give me what I want, then I can tell you what I really want" mode.
- The shorter the cycle of the feedback loop, the more successful the warehouse effort.
- The larger the volume of data that has to be changed, the longer the feedback loop takes.

STRATEGIC CONSIDERATIONS

Figure 9.5 shows that the path of activities that have been described addresses the DSS needs of the organization.

Figure 9.5. The first major path to be followed is the one of DSS.

The data warehouse environment is designed and built for the purpose of supporting the DSS needs of the organization, but there are needs other than DSS needs. Figure 9.6 shows that there are operational needs of the corporation as well.

In Figure 9.6, the operational world is shown as being in a state of chaos. There is much unintegrated data in the operational world. The operational world contains data and systems so old and so patched that they cannot be maintained. The requirements that originally shaped the operational applications have changed into an almost unrecognizable form, and so forth.

The migration plan that has been discussed is solely for the DSS component. But isn't there an opportunity to rectify some or much

Figure 9.6. In order to be successful, the data architect should wait for agents of change to become compelling and ally the efforts toward the architected environment with the appropriate agents.

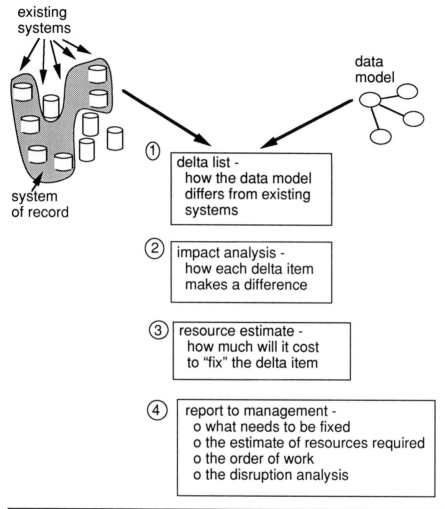

existing
systems

data
model

① delta list -
how the data model
differs from existing
systems

system
of record

② impact analysis -
how each delta item
makes a difference

③ resource estimate -
how much will it cost
to "fix" the delta item

④ report to management -
o what needs to be fixed
o the estimate of resources required
o the order of work
o the disruption analysis

Figure 9.7. The first steps in creating the operational
"clean up" plan.

of the operational "mess" at the same time that the data warehouse
is being built? The answer is that to some extent there is an
opportunity to rebuild less than esthetically pleasing aspects of the
operational environment.

One approach—which is on an independent track of the migration to the data warehouse environment—is to use the data model as a guideline and make a case to management that major changes need to be made to the operational environment. The industry track record of this approach is dismal. The amount of effort, the amount of resources, and the disruption to the end user in undertaking a massive rewrite and restructuring of operational data and systems is such that management seldom supports such an effort with the needed level of commitment and resources.

A better ploy is to coordinate the effort to rebuild operational systems with what is termed the "agents of change":

- the aging of systems
- the radical changing of technology
- organizational upheaval
- massive business changes

When management faces the effects of the agents of change, there is no question that changes will have to be made—the only question is how soon and at what expense. The data architect allies the agents of change with the notion of an architecture and presents management with an irresistible argument for the purpose of restructuring operational processing.

The steps the data architect takes to restructure the operational environment—which is an independent activity of the building of the data warehouse—are shown in Figure 9.7.

First a "delta" list is created. The delta list is an assessment of the differences between the operational environment and the environment depicted by the data model. The delta list is a simple listing, with very little elaboration.

The next step is the impact analysis. At this point an assessment is made of the impact of each item on the delta list. Some items may have a serious impact; other items have a negligible impact on the running of the company.

Next the resource estimate is created. This estimate is for the determination of how many resources will be required to "fix" the delta list item.

Finally, all the above are packaged into a report that goes to information systems management. Management then makes a decision as to what work should proceed, at what pace, and so forth.

METHODOLOGY AND MIGRATION

In the appendix of this book, a methodology for building a data warehouse is described. The methodology is actually a much larger methodology in scope in that it not only contains information as to how to build a data warehouse but it also describes how to use the data warehouse. In addition, the classical activities of operational development are included to form what can be termed a "data driven" methodology.

The methodology described differs from the migration path in several ways. The migration path describes general activities dynamically. The methodology describes specific activities, deliverables from those activities and the order of the activities. But the iterative dynamics of creating a warehouse are not described. In other words, the migration plan describes a sketchy plan in three dimensions, while the methodology describes a detailed plan in one dimension. Together they form a complete picture of what is required to build the data warehouse.

A DATA-DRIVEN DEVELOPMENT METHODOLOGY

There is a universal appeal to development methodologies. Appealing to the intellect, a methodology directs the developer down a rational path, pointing out what needs to be done, in what order, and how long the activity should take. As attractive as the notion of a methodology is, the industry track record has not been good. Across the board, the enthusiasm for methodologies (data warehouse or any other!) has met with disappointment upon implementation. The track record for methodologies put into implementation has generally been a rocky road.

Why have methodologies been a disappointment? There are a plethora of reasons.

• Methodologies generally show a flat, linear flow of activities. In fact, almost any methodology requires execution in terms of iterations. In other words, it is absolutely normal to execute two or three steps, stop, and repeat all or part of those steps again. Methodologies usually don't show or concern themselves with the need to revisit one or more activities. In the case of the data warehouse, this lack of support for iteration makes a methodology a very questionable subject.

- Methodologies usually show activities as occurring once and only once. Indeed, some activities need to be done (successfully!) only once. However, other activities are done repeatedly for different cases (which is a different case than reiteration for refinement).

- Methodologies usually describe a prescribed set of activities to be done. Oftentimes, some of the activities don't need to be done at all, and other activities need to be done that are not shown as part of the methodology, and so forth.

- Methodologies often tell how to do something, not what needs to be done. In describing how to do something, the effectiveness of the methodology becomes mired in detail and in special cases.

- Methodologies often do not distinguish between the sizes of the systems being developed under the methodology. Some systems are so small that a rigorous methodology makes no sense. Some systems are just the right size for a methodology. Other systems are so large that their sheer size and complexity will overwhelm the methodology.

- Methodologies often mix project management concerns with design/development activities to be done. Usually, project management activities should be kept separate from methodological concerns.

- Methodologies often do not make the distinction between operational and DSS processing. The system development life cycles for operational and DSS processing are diametrically opposed in many ways. A methodology must distinguish between operational and DSS processing and development in order to be successful.

- Methodologies often do not include checkpoints and stopping places in the case of failure. "What is the next step if the previous step has not been done properly" is usually not a standard part of a methodology.

- Methodologies are often sold as solutions, not tools. When a methodology is sold as a solution, inevitably the methodology is asked to replace good judgment and common sense, and this is always a mistake.

- Methodologies often generate a lot of paper and very little

design. Design and development activities are not legitimately replaced by paper.
- Methodologies can be very complex, anticipating every possibility that may ever happen, or potentially happen.

Despite these drawbacks, there still is general appeal for methodologies. A general-purpose methodology—applicable to the data driven environment—will be described in this appendix, with full recognition of the pitfalls and track record of methodologies. The data-driven methodology that is outlined owes much to its early predecessors. As such, for a much fuller explanation of the intricacies and techniques described in the methodology, refer to the books listed in references.

One of the salient aspects of a data-driven methodology is that it builds upon previous efforts—building on both code and processes that have been already developed. The only way that development on previous efforts can be achieved is through the recognition of commonality. Before the developer strikes the first line of code or designs the first database, he or she needs to know what already exists and how it affects the development process. A conscious effort must be made to use what is already in place and not reinvent the wheel. That is one of the essences of data-driven development.

DATA-DRIVEN METHODOLOGY

What makes a methodology data driven? How is a data-driven methodology any different from any other methodology? There are at least two distinguishing characteristics of a data driven methodology.

- A data-driven methodology does not take an application-by-application approach to the development of systems. Instead, code and data that have been built previously are built upon, rather than built around. In order to build on previous efforts, the commonality of data and processing must be recognized. Once recognized, data are built upon if it already exists, or if no data exists, data are constructed so that future development may built on it. The key to the recognition of commonality is the data model.

- There is an emphasis on the central store of data—the data warehouse—as the basis for DSS processing, recognizing that DSS processing has a very different development life cycle than operational systems.

SYSTEM DEVELOPMENT LIFE CYCLES

Fundamentally, shaping the data-driven development methodology is the profound difference in the system development life cycles of operational system and DSS systems. Operational development is shaped around a development life cycle that begins with requirements and ends with code. DSS processing begins with data and ends with requirements.

A PHILOSOPHICAL OBSERVATION

In some regards, the best example of methodology is the Boy and Girl Scout merit badge system. The merit badge system is used to determine when a scout is ready to pass on to the next rank. It applies to both country- and city-dwelling boys and girls, the athletically inclined and the intellectually inclined, and to all geographical areas. In short, the merit badge system is a uniform methodology for the measurement of accomplishment that has stood the test of time.

Is there is any secret to the merit badge methodology? If so, it is this: The merit badge methodology does not prescribe *how* any activity is to be accomplished; instead, it merely describes what is to be done with parameters for the measurement of the achievement. The "how to do" that is required is left up to the boy or girl scout.

Philosophically, the approach to methodology that will be described in this paper takes the same perspective as the merit badge system. The results of what must be accomplished and, generally speaking, the order that things must be done in will be described. How the results required are to be achieved is left entirely up to the developer.

OPERATIONAL DEVELOPMENT/DSS DEVELOPMENT

The data-driven methodology will be presented in three parts: METH 1, METH 2, and METH 3. The first part of the methodology—METH 1—is for operational systems and processing. This part of the methodology will probably be most familiar to those used to looking at classically structured operational methodologies. METH 2 is for DSS systems and processing—the data warehouse. The essence of this component of the methodology centers around a data model as the vehicle that allows the commonality of data to be recognized. It is in this section of the appendix that the development of the data warehouse is described. The third part of the methodology—METH 3—describes what occurs in the heuristic component of the development process. It is in METH 3 that the usage of the warehouse is described.

These three sections comprise the data-driven methodology.

SUMMARY

In this chapter, a migration plan and a methodology (found in the appendix) have been described. The migration plan addressed the issues of transforming data out of the existing systems environment into the data warehouse environment. In addition, the dynamics of how the operational environment might be organized was discussed.

A general-purpose data-driven methodology was discussed as well. The general-purpose methodology had three phases—an operational phase, a data warehouse construction phase, and a data warehouse iterative usage phase.

10

A DSS
Design Review
Checklist

One of the most effective techniques for ensuring quality in the operational environment is that of design review. Through design review, errors can be detected and resolved prior to coding. The cost benefit of identifying errors early in the development life cycle is enormous.

In the operational environment, design review is usually done upon completion of the physical design of an application. The types of issues around which an operational design review centers are

- transaction performance,
- batch window adequacy,
- system availability,
- capacity,
- project readiness, and
- user requirements satisfaction.

Done properly in the operational environment, design review can save significant resources and greatly increase user satisfaction. Most importantly, when design review has been properly executed, major pieces of code do not have to be torn up and rewritten after the system has gone into production.

Design review is as applicable to the data warehouse environment as it is to the operational environment, with a few provisos.

One proviso is that systems are developed in the data warehouse environment in an iterative manner, where the requirements are discovered as a part of the development process. The classical operational environment is built under the well-defined SDLC—system development life cycle. Systems in the data warehouse environment are not built under the SDLC. Other differences between the development process in the operational environment and the data warehouse environment are the following:

- Development in the operational environment is done one application at a time. Systems for the data warehouse environment are built a subject area at a time.
- In the operational environment there is a firm set of requirements that form the basis of operational design and development. In the data warehouse environment, there is seldom a firm understanding of processing requirements at the outset of DSS development.
- In the operational environment, transaction response time is a major and burning issue. In the data warehouse environment, transaction response time had better not be an issue.
- In the operational environment, the input from systems usually comes from sources external to the organization, usually from interaction with outside agencies. In the data warehouse environment, it usually comes from systems inside the organization where data is integrated from a wide variety of existing sources.
- In the operational environment, data is nearly all current valued (i.e., data is accurate as of the moment of usage). In the data warehouse environment, data is time variant (i.e., data is relevant to some one moment in time).

There are, then, some substantial differences between the operational and data warehouse environments, and these differences show up in the way design review is conducted.

WHEN TO DO DESIGN REVIEW

Design review in the data warehouse environment is done as soon as a major subject area has been designed and is ready to be added to the data warehouse environment. It does not need to be done for every new database that goes up. Instead, as whole new major subject areas are added to the database, design review becomes an appropriate activity.

Who Should Be in the Design Review?

The attendees at the design review include anyone who has a stake in the development, operation, or usage of the DSS subject area being reviewed.

Normally, this includes

- the DA,
- the DBA,
- programmers,
- the DSS analysts,
- end users other than the DSS analysts,
- operations,
- systems support, and
- management.

Of this group, by far the most important attendees are the end users and the DSS analysts.

One important benefit from having all the parties in the same room together at the same time is the opportunity to short-circuit miscommunications. In an everyday environment where the end user talks to the liaison person who talks to the designer who talks to the programmer, there is ample opportunity for miscommunication and misinterpretation. When all the parties are gathered, there can be direct conversations that are beneficial to the health of the project being reviewed.

What?

The subject for review for the data warehouse environment is any aspect of design, development, project management, or usage that might prevent success. In short, any obstacle to success is relevant to the design review process. As a rule, the more controversial the subject, the more important that it be addressed during the review.

The questions that form the basis of the review process are addressed in the latter part of this chapter.

The Results

There are three results of a data warehouse design review. They are

- an appraisal to management of the issues, and recommendations as to further action,
- a documentation of where the system is in the design, as of the moment of review, and
- an "action item" list that states specific objectives and activities that are a result of the review process.

Administering the Review

The review is led by two people—a facilitator and a recorder. The facilitator is never the manager or the developer of the project being reviewed. If by some chance the facilitator is the project leader, the purpose of the review—from many perspectives—will have been defeated.

To conduct a successful review, it is mandatory that the facilitator be someone removed from the project for the following reasons:

- As an outsider, the facilitator provides an external perspective—a fresh look—at the system. This fresh look often reveals important insights that someone close to the design and development of the system is not capable of providing.
- As an outsider, a facilitator can offer criticism constructively. The criticism that comes from someone close to the development effort is usually taken personally and causes the design review to be reduced to a very base level.

A Typical Data Warehouse Design Review

1. Who is missing in the review? Is any group missing that ought to be in attendance? Are the following groups represented?

- DA
- DBA
- programming
- DSS analysts
- end users

- operations
- systems programming
- auditing
- management

Who is the official representative of each group?

ISSUE: The proper attendance of the design review by the proper people is vital to the success of the review regardless of any other factors. Easily the most important attendee is the DSS analyst or the end user. Management may or may not attend at their discretion.

2. Have the end user requirements been anticipated at all? If so, to what extent have the end user requirements been anticipated? Does the end user representative to the design review agree with the representation of requirements that has been done?

ISSUE: In theory, the DSS environment can be built without interaction with the end user—with no anticipation of end user requirements. However, if there is going to be a need to change the granularity of data in the data warehouse environment, or if EIS/ AI processing is to be built on top of the data warehouse, then some anticipation of requirements is a healthy exercise to go through. As a rule, even when the DSS requirements are anticipated, the level of participation of the end users is very low, and the end result is very sketchy. Furthermore, a large amount of time should not be allocated to the anticipation of end user requirements.

3. How much of the data warehouse has already been built in the data warehouse environment?

- Which subjects?
- How much data—in bytes? In rows? In tracks/cylinders?
- How much processing?
- What growth pattern is there, independent of the project being reviewed?

ISSUE: The current status of the data warehouse environment has a great influence on the development project being reviewed. The very first development effort should be undertaken in a limited scope, trial-and-error basis. There should be little critical processing or data in this phase. In addition, a certain amount of quick feedback and reiteration of development should be anticipated.

Later efforts of data warehouse development will have smaller margins for error.

4. How many major subjects have been identified from the data model? How many are currently implemented? Are fully implemented? Are being implemented by the development project being reviewed? Will be implemented in the foreseeable future?

ISSUE: As a rule, the data warehouse environment is implemented one subject at a time. The first few subjects should be considered almost as experiments. Later subject implementation should reflect the lessons learned from earlier development efforts.

5. Does any major DSS processing (i.e., data warehouse) exist outside the data warehouse environment? If so, what is the chance of conflict or overlap? What migration plan is there for DSS data and processing outside the data warehouse environment? Does the end user understand the migration that will have to occur? What time frame will the migration be done in?

ISSUE: Under normal circumstances, it is a major mistake to have part of the data warehouse environment in the data warehouse environment and other parts out of the data warehouse environment. Only under the most exceptional circumstances should a "split" scenario be allowed. (One of those circumstances is a distributed DSS environment.)

If part of the data warehouse environment in fact does exist outside the data warehouse environment, there should be a plan to bring that part of the DSS world back into the data warehouse environment.

6. Have the major subjects that have been identified been broken down into lower levels of detail?

- Have the keys been identified?
- Have the attributes been identified?
- Have the keys and attributes been grouped together?
- Have the relationships between groupings of data been identified?
- Have the time variances of each group been identified?

ISSUE: There needs to be a data model that serves as the intellectual heart of the data warehouse environment. The data model normally has three levels—a high level model where entities and relationships are identified; a midlevel where keys, attributes, and relationships are identified; and a low level, from where database design can be done. While not all of the data needs to be modelled down to the lowest level of detail in order for the DSS environment to start to be built, at least the high level model must be complete.

7. Is the design discussed in question 6 periodically reviewed? How often? Informally? Formally? What changes occur as a result of the review? How is end user feedback channeled to the developer?

ISSUE: From time to time, the data model needs to be updated to reflect changing business needs of the organization. As a rule, these changes are incremental in nature. It is very unusual to have a revolutionary change. There needs to be an assessment of the impact of these changes on both existing data warehouse data and planned data warehouse data.

8. Has the operational system of record been identified?

- Has the source for every attribute been identified?
- Have the conditions under which one attribute or another will be the source been identified?
- If there is no source for an attribute, have default values been identified?
- Has a common measure of attribute values been identified for those data attributes in the data warehouse environment?
- Has a common encoding structure been identified for those attributes in the data warehouse environment?
- Has a common key structure in the data warehouse environment been identified? Where the system of record key does not meet the conditions for the DSS key structure, has a conversion path been identified?

ISSUE: After the data model has been built, the system of record is identified. The system of record normally resides in the operational environment. The system of record represents the best source of existing data in support of the data model. The issues of integration very much are a factor in defining the system of record.

9. Has the frequency of extract processing—from the operational system of record to the data warehouse environment—been identified? How will the extract processing identify changes to the operational data from the last time an extract process was run?

- By looking at time stamped data?
- By changing operational application code?
- By looking at a log file? An audit file?
- By looking at a "delta" file?
- By rubbing "before" and "after" images together?

ISSUE: The frequency of extract processing is an issue because of the resources required in refreshment, the complexity of refreshment processing, and the need to refresh data on a timely basis. The usefulness of data warehouse data is oftentimes related to how often the data warehouse data is refreshed.

One of the most complex issues—from a technical perspective—is in determining what data is to be scanned for extract processing. In some cases, the operational data that needs to pass from one environment to the next is straightforward. In other cases, it is not clear at all just what data should be examined as a candidate for populating the data warehouse environment.

10. What volume of data will normally be contained in the DSS environment. If the volume of data is large,

- will multiple levels of granularity be specified?
- will data be compacted?
- will data be purged periodically?

ISSUE: In addition to the volumes of data processed by extraction, the designer needs to concern himself/herself with the volume of data actually in the data warehouse environment. The analysis of the volume of data in the data warehouse environment leads directly to the subject of the granularity of data in the data warehouse environment and the possibility of multiple levels of granularity.

11. What data will be filtered out of the operational environment as extract processing is done to create the data warehouse environment?

ISSUE: It is very unusual for all operational data to be passed to the DSS environment. Almost every operational environment contains data that is relevant only to the operational. This data should not be passed to the data warehouse environment.

12. What software will be used to feed the data warehouse environment?

- Has the software been thoroughly shaken out?
- What bottlenecks are there? Might there be?
- Is the interface one-way or two-way?
- What technical support will be required?
- What volume of data will pass through the software?
- What monitoring of the software will be required?
- What alterations to the software will be periodically required?
- What outage will the alterations entail?
- How long will it take to install the software?
- Who will be responsible for the software?
- When will the software be ready for full-blown usage?

ISSUE: The data warehouse environment is capable of handling a large number and types of software interfaces. However, the amount of "break in" time and "infrastructure" time should not be underestimated. The DSS architect must not assume that the linking of the data warehouse environment to other environments will necessarily be straightforward and easy.

13. What software/interface will be required for the feeding of DSS departmental and individual processing out of the data warehouse environment?

- Has the interface been thoroughly tested?
- What bottlenecks might exist?
- Is the interface a one-way or a two-way interface?
- What technical support will be required?
- What traffic of data across the interface is anticipated?
- What monitoring of the interface will be required?
- What alterations to the interface will there be?
- What outage is anticipated as a result of alterations to the interface?
- How long will it take to install the interface?
- Who will be responsible for the interface?
- When will the interface be ready for full-scale utilization?

14. What physical organization of data will be used in the data warehouse environment? Can the data be directly accessed? Sequentially accessed? Can indexes be easily and cheaply created?

ISSUE: The designer needs to review the physical configuration of the data warehouse environment to ensure that adequate capacity will be available and that the data, once in the environment, will be able to be manipulated in a responsive manner.

15. How easy will it be to add more storage to the data warehouse environment at a later point in time? How easy will it be to reorganize data within the data warehouse environment at a later point in time?

ISSUE: No data warehouse is static and no data warehouse is fully specified at the initial moment of design. It is absolutely normal to make corrections in design throughout the life of the data warehouse environment. To construct a data warehouse environment, either where midcourse corrections cannot be made or are awkward to make, is to have a faulty design.

16. What is the likelihood that data in the data warehouse environment will need to be restructured frequently (i.e., columns added, dropped, columns enlarged, keys modified, etc.)? What effect will these activities of restructuring have on ongoing processing in the data warehouse?

ISSUE: Given the volume of data found in the data warehouse environment, restructuring it is not a trivial issue. In addition, with archival data, restructuring after a certain moment in time often becomes a logical impossibility.

17. What are the expected levels of performance in the data warehouse environment? Has a DSS service level agreement been drawn up? Formally? Informally?

ISSUE: Unless a DSS service level agreement has been formally drawn up, it is impossible to measure whether or not performance objectives are being met. The DSS service level agreement should cover both DSS performance levels and down time. Typical DSS service level agreements state such things as

- average performance during peak hours per units of data,
- average performance during off-peak hours per units of data,

- worst performance levels during peak hours per units of data,
- worst performance during off-peak hours per units of data, and
- system availability standards.

One of the difficulties of the DSS environment is measuring performance. Unlike the operational environment where performance can be measured in absolute terms, DSS processing needs to be measured in relation to

- how much processing the individual request is for,
- how much processing is going on concurrently, and
- how many users are on the system at the moment of execution.

18. What are the expected levels of availability? Has an availability agreement been drawn up for the data warehouse environment? Formally? Informally?

ISSUE: (See issue for question 17.)

19. How will the data in the data warehouse environment be indexed or accessed?

- Will any table have more than four indexes?
- Will any table be hashed?
- Will any table have only the primary key indexed?
- What overhead will be required to maintain the index?
- What overhead will be required to load the index initially?
- How often will the index be used?
- Can/should the index be altered to serve a wider usage?

ISSUE: Data in the data warehouse environment needs to be able to be accessed efficiently and in a flexible manner. Unfortunately, the heuristic nature of data warehouse processing is such that the need for indexes is unpredictable. The result is that the accessing of data in the data warehouse environment must not be taken for granted. As a rule, a multi-tiered approach to managing the access of data warehouse data is optimal.

- The hashed/primary key should satisfy most accesses.
- Secondary indexes should satisfy other popular access patterns.
- Temporary indexes should satisfy the occasional access.
- Extraction and subsequent indexing of a subset of data warehouse data should satisfy infrequent or once-in-a-lifetime accesses of data.

In any case, data in the data warehouse environment should not be stored in partitions so large that they cannot be indexed freely.

20. What volumes of processing in the data warehouse environment are to be expected? What about peak periods? What will the profile of the average day look like? The peak rate?

ISSUE: Not only should the volume of data in the data warehouse environment be anticipated, but the volume of processing should be anticipated as well.

21. What level of granularity of data in the data warehouse environment will there be?

- A high level?
- A low level?
- Multiple levels?
- Will rolling summarization be done?
- Will there be a level of "true archival" data?
- Will there be a "living sample" level of data?

ISSUE: Clearly, the most important design issue in the data warehouse environment is that of granularity of data and the possibility of multiple levels of granularity. In a word, if the granularity of the data warehouse environment is done properly, then all other issues become straightforward; if the granularity of data in the data warehouse environment is not designed properly, then all other design issues become complex and burdensome.

22. What purge criteria for data in the data warehouse environment will there be? Will data be truly purged or will it be compacted and archived elsewhere? What legal requirements are there? What audit requirements are there?

ISSUE: Even though data in the DSS environment is archival and of necessity has a low probability of access, it nevertheless has some probability of access (otherwise it should not be stored). When the probability of access reaches zero (or approaches zero), the data needs to be purged. Given that volume of data is one of the most burning issues in the data warehouse environment, purging data that is no longer useful is one of the more important aspects of the data warehouse environment.

23. What total processing capacity requirements are there

- for initial implementation?
- for the data warehouse environment at maturity?

ISSUE: Granted that capacity requirements cannot be planned down to the last bit, it is worthwhile to at least estimate how much capacity will be required, just in case there is a mismatch between needs and what will be available.

24. What relationships between major subject areas will be recognized in the data warehouse environment? Will their implementation

- cause foreign keys to be kept up to date?
- make use of "artifacts"?

What overhead is required in the building and maintenance of the relationship in the data warehouse environment?

ISSUE: One of the most important design decisions the data warehouse designer makes is that of how to implement relationships between data in the data warehouse environment. Data relationships are almost NEVER implemented the same in the data warehouse as they are in the operational environment.

25. Do the data structures internal to the data warehouse environment make use of

- arrays of data?
- selective redundancy of data?
- merging of tables of data?
- creation of commonly used units of derived data?

ISSUE: Even though operational performance is not an issue in the data warehouse environment, performance is nevertheless an issue. The designer needs to consider the design techniques listed above when they can reduce the total amount of I/O consumed. The techniques listed above are classical physical denormalization techniques. Because data is not updated in the data warehouse environment, there are very few restrictions on what can and can't be done.

The factors that determine when one or the other design technique can be used include

- the predictability of occurrences of data,
- the predictability of the pattern of access of data, and
- the need to gather artifacts of data, and so forth.

26. How long will a recovery take? Is operations prepared to execute a full data warehouse database recovery? A partial recovery? Will operations periodically practice recovery so that they will be prepared in the event of a need for recovery? What level of preparedness is exhibited by

- systems support?
- applications programming?
- the DBA?
- the DA?

For each type of problem that can arise, is it clear whose responsibility the problem is?

ISSUE: As in operational systems, the designer must be prepared for the outages that occur during recovery. The frequency of recovery, the length of time required to bring the system back up, and the "domino" effect that can occur during an outage must all be considered.

Have instructions been prepared, tested, and written up? Have these instructions been kept up to date?

27. What level of preparation is there for reorganization/restructuring of

- operations?
- systems support?
- applications programming?
- the DBA?
- the DA?

Have written instructions and procedures been set and tested? Are they up to date? Will they be kept up to date?

ISSUE: See issues for question 26.

28. What level of preparation is there for the loading of a database table by

- operations?
- systems support?

- applications programming?
- the DBA?
- the DA?

Have written instructions and procedures been made and tested? Are they up to date? Will they be kept up to date?

ISSUE: The time and resources for loading can be considerable. This estimation needs to be done carefully and early in the development life cycle.

29. What level of preparation is there for the loading of a database index by

- operations?
- systems support?
- applications programming?
- the DBA?
- the DA?

ISSUE: See the issue for question 28.

30. If there is ever a controversy as to the accuracy of a piece of data in the data warehouse environment, how will the conflict be resolved? Has ownership (or at least source identification) been done for each unit of data in the data warehouse environment? Will ownership be able to be established if the need arises? Who will address the issues of ownership? Who will be the final authority as to the issues of ownership?

ISSUE: Ownership or stewardship of data is an essential component of success in the data warehouse environment. It is inevitable that at some moment in time, the contents of a database will come into question. The designer needs to plan in advance for this eventuality.

31. How will corrections to data be made once date are placed in the data warehouse environment? How frequently will corrections be made? Will corrections be monitored? If there is a pattern of regularly occurring changes, how will corrections at the source (i.e., operational) level be made?

ISSUE: On an infrequent, nonscheduled basis, there may need to be changes made to the data warehouse environment. If there appears a pattern to making changes, then the DSS analyst needs to investigate what is wrong in the operational system.

32. Will public summary data be stored separately from normal primitive DSS data? How much public summary data will there be?

ISSUE: Even though the data warehouse environment contains primitive data, it is normal for there to be public summary data in the data warehouse environment as well. The designer needs to have prepared a logical place for this data to reside.

33. What security requirements will there be for the databases in the data warehouse environment? How will security be enforced?

ISSUE: The access of data becomes an issue, especially as the detailed data becomes summarized or aggregated, where trends become apparent. The designer needs to anticipate the security requirements and prepare the data warehouse environment for them.

34. What audit requirements are there? How will audit requirements be met?

ISSUE: As a rule, system audit can be done at the data warehouse level, but this is almost always a mistake. Instead, detailed record audits are best done at the system of record level.

35. Will compaction of data be used? Has the overhead of compacting/decompacting data been considered? What is the overhead? What is the savings in terms of DASD for compacting/decompacting data?

ISSUE: On the one hand, compaction or encoding of data can save significant amounts of space. On the other hand, both compacting and encoding data require CPU cycles as data is decompacted or decoded upon access. The designer needs to make a thorough investigation of these issues and a deliberate tradeoff in the design.

36. Will encoding of data be done? Has the overhead of encoding/decoding been considered? What, in fact, is the overhead?

ISSUE: See issue for question 35.

37. Will metadata be stored for the data warehouse environment?

ISSUE: Metadata needs to be stored with any archival data as a matter of policy. There is nothing more frustrating than an analyst trying to solve a problem using archival data when the analyst does not know the meaning of the contents of a field being analyzed. This frustration can be alleviated by storing the semantics of data with the data. Over time, it is absolutely normal for the contents and structure of data in the data warehouse environment to change. Keeping track of the changing definition of data is something the designer should ensure is done.

38. Will reference tables be stored in the data warehouse environment?

ISSUE: See issue for question 37.

39. What catalog/dictionary will be maintained for the data warehouse environment? Who will maintain it? How will it be kept up to date? To whom will it be made available?

ISSUE: Not only is keeping track of the definition of data over time an issue, but keeping track of data currently in the data warehouse is important as well.

40. Will update (as opposed to loading and access of data) be allowed in the data warehouse environment? Why? How much? Under what circumstances? On an exception-only basis?

ISSUE: If any updating is allowed on a regular basis in the data warehouse environment, the designer should ask why. The only update that should occur should be on an exception basis and for only small amounts of data. Any exception to this severely compromises the efficacy of the data warehouse environment.

When updates are done (if, in fact, they are done at all), they should be run in a private window when no other processing is done and when there is slack time on the processor.

41. What time lag will there be in getting data from the operational to the data warehouse environment? Will the time lag ever be less than 24 hours? If so, why and under what conditions? Will the passage of data from the operational to the data warehouse environment be a "push" or a "pull" process?

ISSUE: As a matter of policy, any time lag less than 24 hours should be questioned. As a rule, if a time lag of less than 24 hours is required, it is a sign that the developer is building operational requirements into the data warehouse. The flow of data through the data warehouse environment should always be a "pull" process, where data is pulled into the warehouse environment when it is needed, rather than being pushed into the warehouse environment when it is available.

42. What logging of data warehouse activity will be done? Who will have access to the logs?

ISSUE: Most DSS processing does not require logging. If an extensive amount of logging is required, it is usually a sign of lack of understanding of what type of processing is occurring in the data warehouse environment.

43. Will any data other than public summary data flow to the data warehouse environment from the departmental or individual level? If so, describe.

ISSUE: Only on rare occasions should public summary data come from sources other than departmental or individual levels of processing. If much public summary data is coming from other sources, the analyst should ask why.

44. What external data (i.e., data other than that generated by a company's internal sources and systems) will enter the data warehouse environment? Will it be specially marked? Will its source be stored with the data? How frequently will the external data enter the system? How much of it will enter? Will an unstructured format be required? What happens if the external data is found to be inaccurate?

ISSUE: Even though there are legitimate sources of data other than a company's operational systems, if much data are entering externally, the analyst should ask why. Inevitably, there is much less flexibility with the content and regularity of availability of external data, although external data represents an important resource that should not be ignored.

45. What facilities will exist that will help the departmental and the individual user to locate data in the data warehouse environment?

ISSUE: One of the primary features of the data warehouse is ease of accessibility of data. And the first step in the accessibility of data is the initial location of the data.

46. Will there be an attempt to mix operational and DSS processing on the same machine at the same time? Why? How much processing? How much data?

ISSUE: For a multitude of reasons, it makes little sense to mix both operational and DSS processing on the same machine at the same time. Only where there are small amounts of data and small amounts of processing should there be a mixture. But these are not the conditions under which the data warehouse environment is most cost effective. (See the book, *Data Architecture—The Information Paradigm*, QED, for an in-depth discussion of this issue.)

47. How much data will flow back to the operational level from the data warehouse level? At what rate? At what volume? Under what response time constraints? Will the flowback be summarized data or individual units of data?

ISSUE: As a rule, data flows from the operational to the warehouse level to the departmental to the individual levels of processing. There are some notable exceptions. As long as not too much data "back flows," and as long as the back flow is done in a disciplined fashion, there usually is no problem. However, if there is a lot of data that is engaged in back flow, then a red flag should be raised.

48. How much repetitive processing will occur against the data warehouse environment? Will precalculation and storage of derived data save processing time?

ISSUE: It is absolutely normal for the data warehouse environment to have some amount of repetitive processing done against it. If only repetitive processing is done, however, or if no repetitive processing is planned, the designer should question why.

49. How will major subjects be partitioned? By year? By geography? By functional unit? By product line? Just how finely does the partitioning of the data break the data up?

ISSUE: Given the volume of data that is inherent to the data warehouse environment and the unpredictable usage of the data, it is mandatory that data warehouse data be partitioned into physically small units that can be managed independently. The design issue is not whether partitioning is to be done. Instead, the design issue is how partitioning is to be accomplished. In general, partitioning is done at the application level rather than the system level.

The partitioning strategy should be reviewed with the following in mind:

- current volume of data
- future volume of data
- current usage of data
- future usage of data
- partitioning of other data in the warehouse
- usage of other data
- volatility of the structure of data

50. Will sparse indexes be created? Would they be useful?

ISSUE: Sparse indexes created in the right place can save huge amounts of processing. By the same token, sparse indexes require a fair amount of overhead in their creation and maintenance. The designer of the data warehouse environment should consider their use.

51. What temporary indexes will be created? How long will they be kept? How large will they be?

ISSUE: See issue for question 50, except as it applies to temporary indexes.

52. What documentation will there be at the departmental and individual levels? What documentation will there be of the interfaces between the data warehouse environment and the departmental environment? Between the departmental and the individual environment? Between the data warehouse environment and the individual environment?

ISSUE: Given the free-form nature of processing in the departmental and the individual environments, it is unlikely that there will be much in the way of documentation available. However, a documentation of the relationships between the environments is important for the reconcilability of data.

53. Will the user be charged for departmental processing? For individual processing? Who will be charged for data warehouse processing?

ISSUE: It is important that users have their own budgets and be charged for resources used. The instant that processing becomes "free," it is predictable that there will be massive misuse of resources. A charge-back system instills a sense of responsibility in the usage of resources.

54. If the data warehouse environment is to be distributed, have the common parts of the warehouse been identified? How are they to be managed?

ISSUE: In a distributed data warehouse environment, some of the data will necessarily be tightly controlled. The data needs to be identified up front by the designer and metadata controls put in place.

SUMMARY

Design review is an important quality assurance practice that can greatly increase the satisfaction of the user and reduce the development and maintenance costs. Thoroughly reviewing the many aspects of a warehouse environment prior to building the warehouse is a sound practice.

Appendix

DEVELOPING OPERATIONAL SYSTEMS—METH 1

M1—Initial Project Activities

PRECEDING ACTIVITY: Decision to build an operational system.

FOLLOWING ACTIVITY: Preparing to use existing code/data.

TIME ESTIMATE: Indeterminate, depending on size of project.

NORMALLY EXECUTED ONCE OR MULTIPLE TIMES: Once.

SPECIAL CONSIDERATIONS: Because of the ambiguity of this step, it tends to drag out interminably. As long as 90% (or even less) of the system is defined here, the system development should continue into the next phase.

DELIVERABLE: Raw system requirements.

- Interviews—The output of interviews is the "softcore" description of what the system is to do, usually reflecting the opinion of middle management. The format of the output is very freeform. As a rule, the territory covered by interviews is not comprehensive.

- Data gathering—The output from this activity may come from many sources. In general, requirements—usually detailed—that are not caught elsewhere are gathered here. This is a freeform, catchall, requirements-gathering activity, the results of which "fill in the gap" for other requirements-gathering activities.
- JAD (Joint Application Design) session output—The output from these activities is the group "brainstorm" synopsis. One of the benefits of requirements formulation in a JAD session is the spontaneity and flow of ideas, and the critical mass that occurs by having different people in the same room focusing on a common objective. The output of one or more JAD sessions is a formalized set of requirements that collectively represent the end users' needs.
- Strategic business plan analysis—If the company has a strategic business plan, it makes sense to reflect on how the plan relates to the requirements of the system being designed. The influence of the strategic business plan can manifest itself in many ways—in setting growth figures, in identifying new lines of business, in describing organizational changes, and so forth. All of these factors, and more, shape the requirements of the system being built.
- Existing systems shape requirements for a new system profoundly. If related existing systems have been built, at the very least the interface between the new set of requirements and existing systems must be identified.

Conversion, replacement, parallel processing, and so forth are all likely topics. The output of this activity is a description of the impact and influence of existing systems on the requirements for the system being developed.

PARAMETERS OF SUCCESS: When done properly, there is a reduction in the ambiguity of the system, the scope of the development effort is reasonably set, and the components of the system are well organized. The political as well as the technical components of the system should be captured and defined.

M2—Using Existing Code/Data

PRECEDING ACTIVITY: System definition.

FOLLOWING ACTIVITY: Sizing, phasing.

TIME ESTIMATE: Done very quickly, usually in no more than a week in even the largest of designs.

NORMALLY EXECUTED ONCE OR MULTIPLE TIMES: Once.

SPECIAL CONSIDERATIONS: This step is one of the best ways to ensure code reusability and data reusability. This step is crucial to the integration of the environment.

In an architected environment, it is incumbent on every project to

- use as much existing code/data that already exists as possible,
- prepare for future projects that will use code and data to be developed in the project being considered. The output from this step is an identification of existing code/data that can be reused and the steps that need to be taken for future processing.

If existing code/data is to be modified, the modifications are identified as a regular part of the system development requirements. If existing code/data is to be deleted, the deletion becomes a part of the specifications. If conversion of code/data is to be done, the conversion becomes a component of the development effort.

PARAMETERS FOR SUCCESS: To identify what already exists that can be built upon; to identify what needs to be built to prepare for future efforts; to not miss any data/code that is legitimately a building block; to identify all code/data that must be built in recognition of future efforts.

M3—Sizing, Phasing

PRECEDING ACTIVITY: Using existing code/data.

FOLLOWING ACTIVITY: Requirements formalization; capacity analysis.

TIME ESTIMATE: This step goes rapidly, usually in a day or two, even for the largest of designs.

NORMALLY EXECUTED ONCE OR MULTIPLE TIMES: Once, then revisited for each continuing phase of development.

DELIVERABLE: Identification of phases of development.

After the general requirements are gathered, the next step is to size them and divide development up into phases. If the system to be developed is large, it makes sense to break the system into development phases. In doing so, development is parceled out in small, manageable units. Of course, the different development phases must be organized into a meaningful sequence, so that the second phase builds on the first, the third phase builds on the first and second, and so on.

The output from this step is the breakup of general requirements into doable, manageable phases, if the requirements are large enough to require a breakup at all.

PARAMETERS FOR SUCCESS: To continue the development process in increments that are both economic and doable (and for within the political context of the organization as well).

M4—Requirements Formalization

PRECEDING ACTIVITY: Sizing, phasing.

FOLLOWING ACTIVITY: ERD specification; functional decomposition.

TIME ESTIMATE: Indeterminate, depending on size of system, how well the scope of the system has been defined, and how ambiguous the design is up to this point.

NORMALLY EXECUTED ONCE OR MULTIPLE TIMES: Once per phase of development.

DELIVERABLE: Formal requirements specification.

Once the requirements have been gathered, sized, and phased (if necessary), the next step is to formalize them. In this step, the developer ensures that

- the requirements that have been gathered are complete, insofar as it is reasonably possible to gather them;
- the requirements are organized;
- the requirements are readable, comprehensible, and at a low enough level of detail to be effective;
- the requirements are not in conflict with each other;
- the requirements do not overlap; and
- operational and DSS requirements have been separated.

The output from this step is a formal requirements definition that is ready to go to detailed design.

PARAMETERS FOR SUCCESS: A succinct, organized, readable, doable, quantified, complete, usable set of requirements that is able to be used as a document for development.

CA—Capacity Analysis

PRECEDING ACTIVITY: Sizing, phasing.

FOLLOWING ACTIVITY: ERD specification; functional decomposition.

TIME ESTIMATE: Depends on the size of the system being built, but with estimating tools and a focussed planner, two or three weeks is a reasonable estimate for a reasonably sized system.

NORMALLY EXECUTED ONCE OR MULTIPLE TIMES: Once per phase of development.

SPECIAL CONSIDERATIONS: The capacity planning function has a history of confusing issues and including extraneous factors that do not merit special attention. It is important to keep the capacity planning portion of the development process focussed and to the point. Otherwise, the exercise can become a roadblock to progress.

The gross amounts of resources to be consumed by the project being analyzed need to be estimated in this early phase of development. In particular, the following need to be considered:

* DASD consumption
* software requirements (including system software, utilities, special custom code, network software, interface software)
* CPU consumption
* I/O utilization
* main memory requirements
* network/channel utilization

Not only are raw requirements analyzed, but the arrival rate of transactions, peak-period processing, patterns of processing, response time requirements, availability requirements, and mean time to failure requirements are factored in as well.

In addition, if any hardware/software must be ordered, the lead time and the "burn in" time must be accounted for to ensure that proper resources will be in place in time for the application being reviewed.

The output of this phase of development is the assurance that the resources needed to be in place are, in fact, in place.

PARAMETERS FOR SUCCESS: No surprises when it comes to resources being in place when needed, the lead time needed to acquire resources, and the amount of resources needed.

PREQ1—Technical Environment Definition

PRECEDING ACTIVITY: Establishment of the information processing environment.

FOLLOWING ACTIVITY: Sizing, phasing.

TIME ESTIMATE: NA

NORMALLY EXECUTED ONCE OR MULTIPLE TIMES: NA

SPECIAL CONSIDERATIONS: On occasion, it is necessary to build an application system from scratch, including defining the technical environment. If this is the case, the considerations of technical definition are outside the boundaries of the data-driven development methodology.

In order to proceed, it is necessary that the technical environment be defined. If the technical environment is not defined at this point, the result will be much "thrashing." Simply stated, detailed design cannot be meaningfully done until the technical environment is defined.

Certain elements of design beyond this point depend on one or the other technical cornerstones to have been identified. At the least, the following should be established:

- the hardware platform(s) that will be used
- the operating system(s) that will be used
- the DBMS(s) that will be used
- the network software to be used
- the language(s) to be used for development

In addition to what hardware, software, and networking will be used, it is helpful to have established the following as well:

- node residency definition (for network systems)
- management of the system of record

PARAMETERS FOR SUCCESS: A firm, workable, technical definition that will meet the needs of the system being developed.

D1—ERD (Entity Relationship Diagram)

PRECEDING ACTIVITY: Requirements formalization.

FOLLOWING ACTIVITY: Data item set specification.

TIME ESTIMATE: For even the largest of systems, two weeks suffice, if the designers know what they are doing. If they don't know what they are doing, the amount of time required here is indeterminate.

NORMALLY EXECUTED ONCE OR MULTIPLE TIMES: Once.

DELIVERABLE: Identification of major subject areas.

From the general set of formal requirements comes the need to identify the major subjects that will make up the system and the relationship of those major subjects. As a rule, the major subject is at the highest level of abstraction.

Typical major subjects are CUSTOMER, PRODUCT, TRANS-ACTION, and so forth. The relationships of the major subjects are identified, as well as the cardinality of the relationship.

The output of this step is the identification of the major subjects that will make up the system, as well as the relationship of the subjects to each other.

PARAMETERS FOR SUCCESS: All major subjects are identified; all major subjects are identified so that there are no conflicts in domain; all major subjects are identified at the highest level of abstraction.

One major parameter of success is that only primitive data be modelled. Another parameter of success is that the scope of the model be defined prior to starting the ERD modelling.

D2—dis (Data Item Sets)

PRECEDING ACTIVITY: ERD definition.

FOLLOWING ACTIVITY: Performance analysis; data store definition.

TIME ESTIMATE: For each subject area, as long as one month per subject area.

NORMALLY EXECUTED ONCE OR MULTIPLE TIMES: Once for each subject area.

Each subject is further broken down—in terms of level of detail—into a dis (or data item set). The dis contains attributes of data, the grouping of attributes, and keys. In addition, "type of" data is identified. Other structures of data here include connectors—representations of relationships—and secondary groupings of data. The output from this step is the "fleshing out" of the subject areas identified in D1.

PARAMETERS FOR SUCCESS: All types of the major subject are identified; all connectors are correctly identified; all relationships are identified by a connector; all attributes are identified; all attributes are grouped with other attributes that share the same relationship to the key of the grouping of data; all multiply occurring groups of attributes are separated from singularly occurring groups of attributes; all recursive relationships are designed in the most general case necessary. Only primitive data is found here. Derived data is identified, stored, and managed elsewhere.

D3—Performance Analysis

PRECEDING ACTIVITY: Data item set development.

FOLLOWING ACTIVITY: Physical database design.

TIME ESTIMATE: One week per subject area, unless the subject area is huge.

NORMALLY EXECUTED ONCE OR MULTIPLE TIMES: Once per subject area.

SPECIAL CONSIDERATIONS: This step does not need to be done in the case of small amounts of data and/or small amounts of processing.

This step is performed if the volume of data, the volume of processing, the traffic over the network, the growth of data and processing, or the peak period of processing will produce significant amounts of activity. If none of those factors will occur, this step is not done.

In this step, the issue of physical denormalization of data is addressed. Specifically, the design practices of

- merging tables,
- selective introduction of redundancy,
- creating popular pools of derived data,
- creating arrays of data, and
- further separation of data where there is a wide disparity in the probability of access of data is considered.

If this activity is done at all, the output reflects a much more streamlined design, with little or no loss of the benefits of normalization of data.

PARAMETERS FOR SUCCESS: A design that will be efficient to access and update, both in terms of data and programs that access and update data. Done properly, this step insures efficient resource utilization.

D4—Physical Database Design

PRECEDING ACTIVITY: Performance analysis.

FOLLOWING ACTIVITY: Pseudocode development.

TIME ESTIMATE: One day per table to be designed.

NORMALLY EXECUTED ONCE OR MULTIPLE TIMES: Once per table.

SPECIAL CONSIDERATIONS: If the input to this step is incorrect or ambiguous, the amount of work required here can be much more than that estimated.

DELIVERABLE: Tables, databases physically designed.

Now the output from D3 and/or D4 is used to produce a physical database design. Some of the characteristics of the output include

- indexing,
- physical attribution of data,
- partitioning strategies,
- designation of keys,
- clustering/interleaving,
- management of variable-length data,
- NULL/NOT NULL specification, and
- referential integrity.

The output of this step is the actual specification of the database to the DBMS, or whatever data management software/conventions are adopted.

PARAMETERS OF SUCCESS: Done properly, this stage of analysis transforms all the considerations of logical design of data, performance, update, access, availability, reorganization, restructuring of data, etc., into a workable database design.

P1—Functional Decomposition

PRECEDING ACTIVITY: Requirements formalization.

FOLLOWING ACTIVITY: Context level 0 specification.

TIME ESTIMATE: Depends on size of system and degree of ambiguity (and how firmly and unambiguously the scope has been established). As a rule, two weeks for a reasonably sized system is adequate.

NORMALLY EXECUTED ONCE OR MULTIPLE TIMES: Once per phase of development.

From the requirements document comes the functional decomposition. The functional decomposition merely takes the broad function accomplished by the system and breaks it down into a series of succeedingly smaller functions (down to a level sometimes called the "primitive" level).

The output of this process is a large functional decomposition describing the different activities to be performed from a high level to a low level.

PARAMETERS OF SUCCESS: Reflected entirely and only are the functions to be designed. Factored into the step are the considerations of other functions that have served or will serve as building blocks. Done properly, this step produces a document that is comprehensible, organized, readable, and complete.

P2—Context Level 0

PRECEDING ACTIVITY: Functional decomposition.

FOLLOWING ACTIVITY: Context level 1-n specification.

TIME ESTIMATE: Three days.

NORMALLY EXECUTED ONCE OR MULTIPLE TIMES: Once per phase.

Context level 0 of the functional decomposition describes, at the highest level of abstraction, the major activities to be developed. Context level 0 for process specification corresponds to the ERD in data modelling.

PARAMETERS FOR SUCCESS: Done well, the major activities of the system, and ONLY the major activities of the system, and how they relate are identified in this document.

P3—Context Level 1-n

PRECEDING ACTIVITY: Context level 0 specification.

FOLLOWING ACTIVITY: DFD specification.

TIME ESTIMATE: One day per function.

NORMALLY EXECUTED ONCE OR MULTIPLE TIMES: Once per function.

DELIVERABLE: Complete functional decomposition (Note: multiple steps contribute to this deliverable).

The remaining levels of the functional decomposition describe the more detailed activities that occur. Context levels 1-n correspond, in terms of process design, to the data item set (the dis), in terms of data design.

PARAMETERS FOR SUCCESS: When this step has been done properly, all major activities are broken down to a primitive level. The breakdown is orderly, organized, complete, and in accordance with the flow of activity.

P4—Data Flow Diagram (dfd)

PRECEDING ACTIVITY: Context level 1-n specification.

FOLLOWING ACTIVITY: Algorithmic specification.

TIME ESTIMATE: One hour per activity (at a primitive level).

NORMALLY EXECUTED ONCE OR MULTIPLE TIMES: Once per activity.

DELIVERABLE: Data flow diagram for each process.

At each context level n—the primitive level—a dfd is drawn. The dfd indicates the input to a process, the output of a process, the data stores needed to establish the process, and a brief description of the process. A dfd may be done for context levels higher than n if it turns out that a program or process is likely to be written for that context level.

PARAMETERS FOR SUCCESS: The input and output for every primitive activity is identified, and the flow of activity identified as well. Data stores are outlined, and the work to be done by each activity is specified.

P5—Algorithmic Specification; Performance Analysis

PRECEDING ACTIVITY: DFD specification.

FOLLOWING ACTIVITY: Pseudocode.

TIME ESTIMATE: Varies, from five minutes to two days per activity at the primitive level that must be specified.

NORMALLY EXECUTED ONCE OR MULTIPLE TIMES: Once per activity.

The processes that are defined by the dfd for primitives are further broken down into detailed algorithmic specification. In other words, in this step, the actual processing to occur step by step is outlined.

In addition, if performance is to be an issue, the effect of performance on program design is factored in. Such design techniques as the following are considered here:

- breaking a long running program into a series of shorter running programs
- requiring a program to access a smaller amount of data
- shortening the time a unit of data is locked
- changing a lock from update potential to access only

PARAMETERS FOR SUCCESS: Algorithmic specification is done well when all details needed for specification are identified, only details needed for specification are identified, and the specification of algorithmic is specified, one step at a time, including all possibilities. In addition, conformance to the standard work unit (SWU) is ensured here.

P6—Pseudocode

PRECEDING ACTIVITY: Algorithmic specification; physical database design; data store design.

FOLLOWING ACTIVITY: Coding.

TIME ESTIMATE: Varies (see previous activity).

NORMALLY EXECUTED ONCE OR MULTIPLE TIMES: Once per activity (at the primitive level).

The algorithms and program specifications are further refined into pseudocode. The designer ensures that all needed data for processing is available. All variables used in calculations, transformations, updates, etc., are identified here. Any loose ends are identified. Performance at the design level is considered here. The output of this activity is coding specifications ready for actual code.

PARAMETERS FOR SUCCESS: The final pass at programming specification includes

- completeness
- order of execution
- all cases required
- all contingencies, including error handling and exception conditions
- structure of coding

P7—Coding

PRECEDING ACTIVITY: Pseudocode.

FOLLOWING ACTIVITY: Walkthrough.

TIME ESTIMATE: Depends, from one day per activity to two weeks per activity.

NORMALLY EXECUTED ONCE OR MULTIPLE TIMES: Once per activity.

DELIVERABLE: Source code.

The pseudocode is translated into source code. If the data has been designed properly, and if the specification of pseudocode has been thorough, this step goes smoothly. The output of this step is source code.

PARAMETERS OF SUCCESS: The complete and efficient translation of pseudocode into code, including inline documentation. Done properly, all requirements previously identified are satisfied by this point.

P8—Walkthrough

PRECEDING ACTIVITY: Coding.

FOLLOWING ACTIVITY: Compilation.

TIME ESTIMATE: One hour per activity.

NORMALLY EXECUTED ONCE OR MULTIPLE TIMES: Once per activity.

The walkthrough is the verbal explanation of code in front of peers. The intent is to find coding errors (or any other kind) before testing. The output of this step is code that has been publicly aired and is as free from error as possible.

PARAMETERS FOR SUCCESS: The detection of errors prior to coding. When this step has been done properly, there will be very few errors left to be found by other means.

P9—Compilation

PRECEDING ACTIVITY: Walkthrough.

FOLLOWING ACTIVITY: Unit testing; stress testing.

TIME ESTIMATE: One hour or less per activity.

NORMALLY EXECUTED ONCE OR MULTIPLE TIMES: Until a clean compile is achieved.

Source code is run through the compiler. All errors found in compilation are corrected. The output of this step is compiled code, ready to be tested.

PARAMETERS FOR SUCCESS: Compiled code that is ready for testing.

P10—Unit Testing

PRECEDING ACTIVITY: Compilation.

FOLLOWING ACTIVITY: Implementation.

METH 1

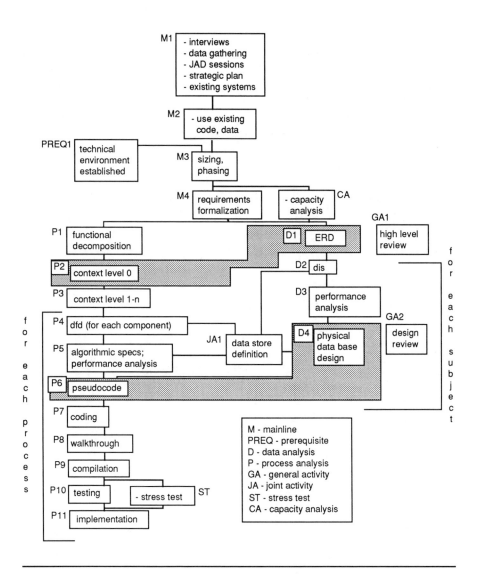

TIME ESTIMATE: Varies widely.

NORMALLY EXECUTED ONCE OR MULTIPLE TIMES: Varies.

Compiled code is tested. There are several levels of unit testing. The simplest (lowest) level of unit testing occurs when the compiled module is tested by itself, ensuring that the function it does is satisfactory. Next, the compiled code is added to other code with which the compiled code will have to work. New levels of unit testing occur in order to ensure the integration of the compiled code with other modules that will be interfaced. A third level of unit testing occurs when major groups of modules are ready to be tested together.

The output of this step is tested code, ready for execution.

PARAMETERS FOR SUCCESS: When executed properly, the code that passes on to the next step has program logic correctly specified. Furthermore, all conditions are tested before code is passed to the next stage, including error and exception conditions.

P11—Implementation

PRECEDING ACTIVITY: Unit test; stress test.

FOLLOWING ACTIVITY: NA

TIME ESTIMATE: NA

There are many activities in implementation. To some extent, implementation is an ongoing activity that has no end. Some of the typical activities of implementation are

- training, indoctrination
- loading of programs
- initial loading of data
- conversions of data, if necessary
- monitoring utilities established
- writing documentation
- recovery, reorg procedures established

The output of this step (if in fact there really is an end to the step!) is a satisfactorily running system.

PARAMETERS FOR SUCCESS: When this step (if in fact it really is a step) is done, the result is a happy user.

DELIVERABLE: A system that satisfies specifications.

DATA WAREHOUSE DEVELOPMENT—METH 2

DSS1—Data Model Analysis

PRECEDING ACTIVITY: The commitment to build a data warehouse.

FOLLOWING ACTIVITY: Subject area analysis; breadbox analysis; data warehouse design.

TIME ESTIMATE: Varies widely, depending on the status and quality of the data model.

NORMALLY EXECUTED ONCE OR MULTIPLE TIMES: Once.

At the outset, a data model needs to have been defined. The data model needs to have

- identified the major subject areas
- the boundaries of the model clearly defined
- separated primitive from derived data
- identified for each subject area
  - keys
  - attributes
  - groupings of attributes
  - relationships among groupings of attributes
  - multiply occurring data
  - "type of" data

The output from this step is a confirmation that the organization has built a solid data model. If the model does not meet the criteria specified, then progress should be halted until the model is brought up to standards of quality.

PARAMETERS FOR SUCCESS: The data model will have

- major subjects identified
- each major subject with its own separate definition of data, including
  - subtypes of data
  - attributes of data
  - relationships of data clearly defined
  - groupings of data defined
  - keys defined

In addition, each group of data that will go into the data warehouse will have DSS data and operational-only data delineated. All DSS data will have its own time-variant key specified, usually as the lower order of a higher key.

DSS2—Breadbox Analysis

PRECEDING ACTIVITY: Data model analysis.

FOLLOWING ACTIVITY: Data warehouse database design.

TIME ESTIMATE: From one day to two weeks, depending on how well the scope has been defined, how well the data model has been defined, etc.

NORMALLY EXECUTED ONCE OR MULTIPLE TIMES: Once.

DELIVERABLE: Granularity analysis.

Once the model has been analyzed as brought up to a level of sufficient quality, the next step is to do "bread box" analysis. Bread box analysis is a sizing—in terms of gross estimates—of the DSS environment. If volume of data is going to be a problem, it is important to know at the outset. Bread box analysis simply projects—in raw terms—how much data the data warehouse will hold.

The output of bread box analysis is simple—if the data warehouse is to contain large amounts of data, then multiple levels of granularity need to be considered. If the data warehouse is not to contain a massive amount of data, then there is no need to plan the design for multiple levels of granularity.

PARAMETERS FOR SUCCESS: An estimate of the amount of data—in terms of number of rows—both on the one-year horizon and on the five-year horizon for the entire data warehouse environment, is the result of the process. Based on the results of the estimate, the issue of whether different levels of granularity are needed is decided. If multiple levels of granularity are needed, exactly what those levels are is a part of the output of this step.

DSS3—Technical Assessment

PRECEDING ACTIVITY: The commitment to build a data warehouse.

FOLLOWING ACTIVITY: Technical environment preparation.

TIME ESTIMATE: One week.

NORMALLY EXECUTED ONCE OR MULTIPLE TIMES: Once.

DELIVERABLE: Technical environment assessment.

The technical requirements for managing the data warehouse are very, very different from the technical requirements and consideration for managing data and processing in the operational environment. That is why a separate, central store of DSS data is so popular.

PARAMETERS OF SUCCESS: When executed properly, the technical definition of the data warehouse satisfies the following criteria:

- ability to manage large amounts of data
- ability to allow data to be accessed flexibly
- ability to organize data according to a data model
- ability both to receive and send data to a wide variety of technologies
- ability to have data loaded en masse periodically
- ability to access data set at a time or record at a time

DSS4—Technical Environment Preparation

PRECEDING ACTIVITY: Technical assessment.

FOLLOWING ACTIVITY: Data warehouse design; population.

TIME ESTIMATE: One week to one month.

NORMALLY EXECUTED ONCE OR MULTIPLE TIMES: Once.

Once the architectural configuration for the data warehouse has been established, the next step is to identify technically how the configuration can be accommodated. Some of the typical issues that must be addressed here are

- what amount of DASD is required;
- what link—either across the network or into the network—will be required;
- what volume of processing is anticipated;
- how to minimize and/or alleviate conflicts of processing between competing access programs;

- what volume of traffic will be generated coming out of the technology that controls the data warehouse;
- what is the nature of traffic—either short or long bursts—coming out of the technology that controls the data warehouse.

PARAMETERS FOR SUCCESS: When this step has been done properly, there are no technical barriers to success. The technical components that must have been installed, allocated, "burned in," and ready to receive data include

- the network,
- DASD,
- the operating system managing DASD,
- the interface to and from the warehouse,
- the software used to manage the data warehouse, and
- data warehouse.

DSS5—Subject Area Analysis

PRECEDING ACTIVITY: Data model analysis.

FOLLOWING ACTIVITY: Source system analysis.

TIME ESTIMATE: One day.

NORMALLY EXECUTED ONCE OR MULTIPLE TIMES: Once per population project.

DELIVERABLE: Which subject area to build next.

Now the subject area to be populated is selected. The first subject area to be selected must be large enough to be meaningful and small enough to be able to be implemented. If by some chance a subject area is truly large and complex, a subset of the subject area may be chosen for implementation. The output from this step is a scope of effort in terms of a subject.

PARAMETERS FOR SUCCESS: The output from this phase when done well is a definition of what data is to be populated next. In the first few populations, small subjects are usually selected. In later populations, larger subjects, or even subsets of subjects are selected. When done properly, the subject selected for population meets the needs of the stage of development of the data warehouse.

DSS6—Data Warehouse Design

PRECEDING ACTIVITY: Data model analysis; source system analysis; breadbox analysis.

FOLLOWING ACTIVITY: Program specification.

TIME ESTIMATE: One week to three weeks.

NORMALLY EXECUTED ONCE OR MULTIPLE TIMES: Once.

DELIVERABLE: Physical database design for the warehouse.

The data warehouse is designed based on the data model. Some of the characteristics of the ultimate design include

- an accommodation of the different levels of granularity, if indeed there are multiple levels of granularity;
- an orientation of data to the major subjects of the corporation;
- the presence of only primitive data and publicly derived data;
- the absence of non-DSS data;
- time variancy of every record of data;
- physical denormalization of data where applicable (i.e., where performance warrants); and
- creation of data "artifacts" where relationships of data that once were in the operational environment are brought over to the data warehouse.

The output of this step is a physical database design of the data warehouse. Note that not all of the data warehouse needs to be designed in detail at the outset. It is entirely acceptable to design in detail at the outset. It is entirely acceptable to design the major structures of the data warehouse initially, then fill in the details at a later point in time.

PARAMETERS FOR SUCCESS: When this step is done properly, the result is a data warehouse that

- has a manageable amount of data,
- can be loaded in a reasonable fashion,
- can be accessed in a reasonable fashion, and
- can be indexed and searched in a reasonably efficient fashion.

DSS7—Source System Analysis

PRECEDING ACTIVITY: Subject area analysis.

FOLLOWING ACTIVITY: Program specification; data warehouse design.

TIME ESTIMATE: One week per subject area.

NORMALLY EXECUTED ONCE OR MULTIPLE TIMES: Once per subject area.

DELIVERABLE: Identification of the system of record.

Once the subject to be populated is identified, the next activity is to identify the source data for the subject in the existing systems environment. It is absolutely normal for there to be a variety of sources of data for DSS data. It is at this point that the issues of integration are addressed. The following represents the issues to be addressed here:

- key structure/key resolution as data passes from the operational environment to the DSS environment
- attribution
  - what to do when there are multiple sources to choose from
  - what to do when there are no sources to choose from
  - what transformations—encoding/decoding, conversions, etc.—must be made as data is selected for transport to the DSS environment
- how time variancy will be created from current value data
- structure—how the DSS structure will be created from the operational structure
- relationships—how operational relationships will appear in the DSS environment

The output of this step is the mapping of data from the operational environment to the DSS environment.

PARAMETERS FOR SUCCESS: When done properly, the source system that serves the needs of the data warehouse uses

- timely data
- complete data
- accurate data
- data that conforms to the structure of the data warehouse needs

- data that is near to the source
- data that is efficient to access

DSS8—Specifications

PRECEDING ACTIVITY: Source system analysis; data warehouse design.

FOLLOWING ACTIVITY: Programming.

TIME ESTIMATE: One week per extract/integration program.

NORMALLY EXECUTED ONCE OR MULTIPLE TIMES: Once for each program that needs to be written.

Once the interface between the operational and the DSS environment has been outlined, the next step is to formalize the interface in terms of program specifications. Some of the major issues here include the following:

- How do I know what operational data to scan?
    - Is the operational data time stamped?
    - Is there a "delta" file?
    - Are there system logs/audit logs that can be used?
    - Can existing source code and data structure be changed to create a "delta" file?
    - Do "before" and "after" image files have to be rubbed together?
- How do I know how to store the output, once scanned?
    - Is the DSS data preallocated, preformatted?
    - Is data appended?
    - Is data replaced?
    - Are updates in the DSS environment made?

The output from this step is the actual program specifications that will be used to bring data over from the operational environment to the data warehouse.

PARAMETERS FOR SUCCESS: When done properly, this step allows the extract and integration of data to be done as efficiently and as simply as possible. Note that seldom is this a smooth, simple process.

DSS9—Programming

PRECEDING ACTIVITY: Specification.

FOLLOWING ACTIVITY: Population.

TIME ESTIMATE: One week per extract/integration program.

NORMALLY EXECUTED ONCE OR MULTIPLE TIMES: Once per program.

DELIVERABLE: Extract, integration, time-perspective program transformation.

This step includes all the standard activities of programming, such as the following:

- development of pseudocode
- coding
- compilation
- walkthroughs
- testing—unit, stress—in its many forms

PARAMETERS FOR SUCCESS: When done properly, code that is generated out of this step is

- efficient,
- documented,
- able to be changed easily,
- accurate,
- complete.

DSS10—Population

PRECEDING ACTIVITY: Programming; technical environment preparation.

FOLLOWING ACTIVITY: Usage of the data warehouse.

TIME ESTIMATE: NA

NORMALLY EXECUTED ONCE OR MULTIPLE TIMES: NA

DELIVERABLE: Usable data warehouse.

This step entails nothing more than the execution of the DSS programs previously developed. The issues addressed here are the following:

- the frequency of population
- purging populated data

- "aging" populated data (i.e., running tallying summary programs)
- managing multiple levels of granularity
- refreshing living sample data, if in fact living sample tables have been built

The output of this step is a populated, functional data warehouse.

PARAMETERS FOR SUCCESS: When done properly, the result is an accessible, understandable warehouse that serves the needs of the DSS community.

HEURISTIC PROCESSING

The third phase of development in the architected environment is the usage of data warehouse data for the purpose of analysis. Once the data in the data warehouse environment is populated, usage may commence.

There are several essential differences in the development that occurs at this level and development in other parts of the environment. The first major difference in development here is that the development process always starts with data, i.e., the data in the data warehouse. The second difference is that requirements are not known at the start of the development process. The third difference (which is really a by-product of the first two factors) is that processing is done in a very iterative, very heuristic fashion. In other types of development, there is always a certain amount of iteration. But in the DSS component of development that occurs after the data warehouse is developed, the whole nature of iteration changes. Iteration of processing is a normal and essential part of the analytical development process, much more so than it is elsewhere.

The steps taken in the DSS development components can be divided into two categories—the repetitively occurring analysis (or, as it is sometimes called, the "departmental" or "functional" analysis) and the true heuristic processing (or the "individual" level).

METH 3 shows the steps of development to be taken after the data warehouse has begun to be populated.

METH 2

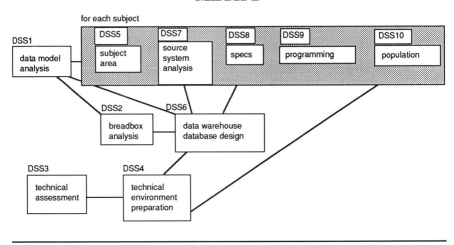

for each subject

DSS1 — data model analysis

DSS5 — subject area
DSS7 — source system analysis
DSS8 — specs
DSS9 — programming
DSS10 — population

DSS2 — breadbox analysis
DSS6 — data warehouse database design

DSS3 — technical assessment
DSS4 — technical environment preparation

METH 3

DEPT1

- for departmental, repetitive reports | standard requirements development for reports |

- for heuristic analytical processing

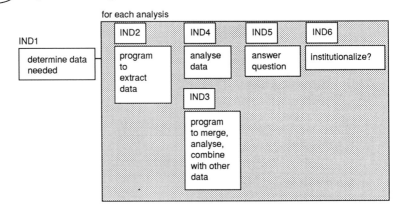

for each analysis

IND1 — determine data needed

IND2 — program to extract data
IND4 — analyse data
IND5 — answer question
IND6 — institutionalize?

IND3 — program to merge, analyse, combine with other data

HEURISTIC DSS DEVELOPMENT—METH 4

DEPT1—Repeat Standard Development—For repetitive analytical processing (usually called delivering standard reports), the normal requirements-driven processing occurs. This means that the following steps (described earlier) are repeated:

M1—interviews, data gathering, JAD, strategic plan, existing systems
M2—sizing, phasing
M3—requirements formalization
P1—functional decomposition
P2—context level 0
P3—context level 1-n
P4—dfd for each component
P5—algorithmic specification; performance analysis
P6—pseudocode
P7—coding
P8—walkthrough
P9—compilation
P10—testing
P11—implementation

In addition, at least part of the following will occur at the appropriate time:

GA1—high-level review
GA2—design review

It does not make sense to do the data analysis component of development because the developer is working from the data warehouse.

The output of this activity is reports that are produced on a regular basis.

PARAMETERS FOR SUCCESS: When done properly, this step ensures that regular report needs are met. These needs usually include

- regulatory reports,
- accounting reports,
- key factor indicator reports,

- marketing reports, and
- sales reports.

Information needs that are predictable and repetitive are met by this function.

NOTE: For highly iterative processing, there are parameters of success, but they are met collectively by the process. Since requirements are not defined a priori, the parameters of success for each iteration are somewhat subjective.

IND1—Determine Data Needed

At this point, data in the data warehouse is selected for potential usage in the satisfaction of reporting requirements. While the developer works from an educated guess perspective, it is understood that the first two or three times this activity is initiated, only some of the data needed will be retrieved.

The output from this activity is data selected for further analysis.

IND2—Program to Extract Data

Once the data for analytical processing is selected, the next step is to write a program to access and strip the data. The program written should be able to be modified easily because it is anticipated that the program will be run, modified, then rerun on numerous occasions.

DELIVERABLE: Data pulled from the warehouse for DSS analysis.

IND3—Combine, Merge, Analyze

After data has been selected, it is prepared for analysis. Oftentimes this means

- editing the data,
- combining with other data, and
- refining the data.

Like all other heuristic processes, it is anticipated that this program be written so that it is easily modifiable and able to be rerun quickly. The output of this activity is data fully usable for analysis.

DELIVERABLE: Analysis with other relevant data.

IND4—Analyze Data

Once data has been selected and prepared, the question is "Do the results obtained meet the needs of the analyst?" If the results are not met, another iteration occurs. If the results are met, then the final report preparation is begun.

DELIVERABLE: Fulfilled requirements.

IND5—Answer Question

The final report that is produced is often the result of many iterations of processing. Very seldom is the final conclusion the result of a single iteration of analysis.

IND6—Institutionalization

The final issue to be decided is whether the final report that has been created should be institutionalized. If there is a need to run the report repetitively, it makes sense to submit the report as a set of requirements and to rebuild the report as a regularly occurring operation.

SUMMARY

How the different activities relate and how the activities relate to the notion of data architecture are described by the diagram shown in METH 4.

METH 4

DATA DRIVEN
DEVELOPMENT METHODOLOGY

DSS SECTOR

OPERATIONAL SECTOR

DATA WAREHOUSE

DEPARTMENTAL

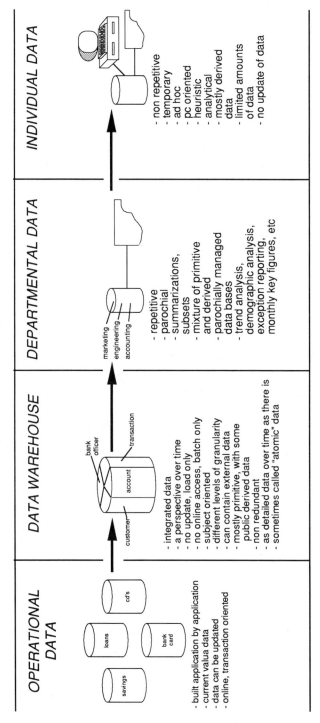

DATA ARCHITECTURE

OPERATIONAL DATA

savings
loans
bank card
cd's

- built application by application
- current valua data
- data can be updated
- online, transaction oriented

DATA WAREHOUSE

customer
account
bank officer
transaction

- integrated data
- a perspective over time
- no update, load only
- no online access, batch only
- subject oriented
- different levels of granularity
- can contain external data
- mostly primitive, with some public derived data
- non redundant
- as detailed data over time as there is
- sometimes called "atomic" data

DEPARTMENTAL DATA

marketing
engineering
accounting

- repetitive
- parochial
- summarizations, subsets
- mixture of primitive and derived
- parochially managed data bases
- trend analysis, demographic analysis, exception reporting, monthly key figures, etc

INDIVIDUAL DATA

- non repetitive
- temporary
- ad hoc
- pc oriented
- heuristic
- analytical
- mostly derived data
- limited amounts of data
- no update of data

SELECTED TOPICS

The best way to describe the data-driven nature of the development methodology is graphically. Figure METH 5 shows that the data model is at the heart of the data-driven methodology.

The data model relates to the design of operational data, to the design of data in the data warehouse, to the development and design process for operational data, and for the development and design process for the data warehouse. Figure METH 5 shows how the same data model relates to each of those activities and databases.

The data model is the key to identifying commonality across applications. One might ask, what about the commonality of processing? Isn't it important to recognize the commonality of processing as well?

The answer is that of course it is important to recognize the commonality of processing across applications. But there are several problems with trying to focus on the commonality of processes—processes change much more rapidly than data, processes tend to mix common and unique processing so tightly that they are often inseparable, and classical process analysis often places an artificially small boundary on the scope of the design. Data is inherently more stable than processing. The scope of a data analysis is easier to enlarge than the scope of a process model. Therefore, focussing upon data as the keystone for recognizing commonality makes sense. In addition, the assumption is made that if commonality of data is discovered, the discovery will lead to a corresponding commonality of processing.

For these reasons, the data model—which cuts across all applications and reflects the corporate perspective—is the foundation for identifying and unifying commonality of data and processing.

Deliverables

The steps of the data-driven development methodology include a deliverable. In truth, some steps contribute to a deliverable with other steps. For the most part, however, each step of the methodology has its own unique deliverable.

The deliverables of the process analysis component of the development of operational systems are shown by Figure METH 6.

METH 5

DATA WAREHOUSE

- integrated data
- a perspective over time
- no update, load only
- no online access, batch only
- subject oriented
- different levels of granularity
- can contain external data
- mostly primitive, with some public derived data
- non redundant
- as detailed data over time as there is
- sometimes called "atomic" data

OPERATIONAL DATA

- built application by application
- current valua data
- data can be updated
- online, transaction oriented

DSS1 data model analysis
DSS2 breadbox analysis
DSS3 technical assessment
DSS4 technical environment preparation
DSS5 subject area
DSS6 data warehouse database design
DSS7 source system analysis
DSS8 specs
DSS9 programming
DSS10 population

for each subject

data model

PREO1 technical environment established

M1 - interviews / - data gathering / - JAD sessions / - strategic plan / - existing systems
M2 - use existing code, data
M3 sizing, phasing
M4 requirements formalization

P1 functional decomposition
P2 context level 0
P3 context level 1-n
P4 dfd (for each component)
P5 algorithmic specs; performance analysis
P6 pseudocode
P7 coding
P8 walkthrough
P9 compilation
P10 testing
P11 implementation

JA1 data store definition

GA1 high level review
GA2 design review

CA - capacity analysis

D1 ERD
D2 dis
D3 performance analysis
D4 physical data base design

ST - stress test

M - mainline
PREQ - prerequisite
D - data analysis
P - process analysis
GA - general activity
JA - joint activity
ST - stress test
CA - capacity analysis

for each subject

for each process

235

METH 6

DELIVERABLES THROUGHOUT THE DEVELOPMENT LIFE CYCLE

Figure METH 6 shows that the deliverable for the interview and data-gathering process is a raw set of systems requirements. The analysis to determine what code/data can be reused and the step for sizing/phasing the raw requirements contribute a deliverable describing the phases of development.

The activity of requirements formalization produces (not surprisingly!) a formal set of system specifications. The result of the functional decomposition activities is the deliverable of a complete functional decomposition.

The deliverable for the dfd definition is a set of dfd's that describe the functions that have been decomposed. In general, the dfd's represent the primitive level of decomposition.

The activity of coding produces the deliverable of programs. And finally, the activity of implementation produces a completed system.

The deliverables for data analysis for operational systems are shown in Figure METH 7.

The same deliverables discussed earlier are produced by the interview and data gathering process, the sizing and phasing activity, and the definition of formal requirements.

The deliverable of the ERD activity is the identification of the major subject areas and their relationship to each other. The deliverable of the dis activity is the fully attributed and normalized description of each subject area. The final deliverable of physical database design is the actual table or database design, ready to be defined to the database management system(s).

The deliverables of the data warehouse development effort are shown first by Figure METH 8.

Figure METH 8 shows that the result of the breadbox analysis is the granularity and volume analysis. The deliverable associated with data warehouse database design is the physical design of data warehouse tables. The deliverable associated with technical environment preparation is the establishment of the technical environment in which the data warehouse will exist. Note that this environment may or may not be the same environment in which operational systems exist.

On a repetitive basis, the deliverables of data warehouse population activities are represented by Figure METH 9.

Figure METH 9 shows that the deliverable for subject area analysis—each time the data warehouse is to be populated—is the selection of a subject (or possibly a subset of a subject) for population.

METH 7

DELIVERABLES FOR OPERATIONAL DATA ANALYSIS

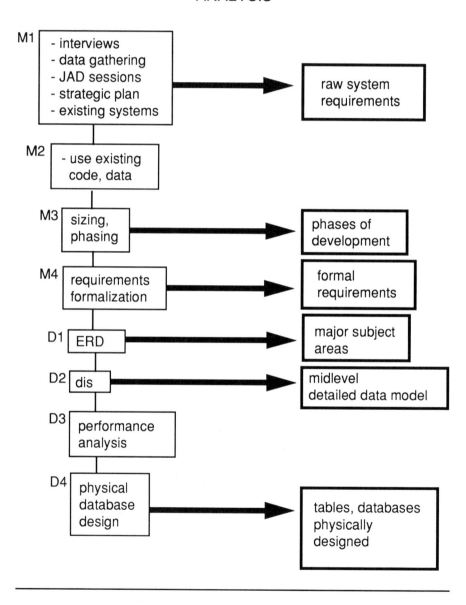

METH 8

PRELIMINARY DATA WAREHOUSE DELIVERABLES

DSS2
breadbox analysis

granularity analysis

DSS6
data warehouse database design

physical database design

DSS4
technical environment preparation

DSS technical environment ready for loading

METH 9

DELIVERABLES FROM THE STEPS OF DATA WAREHOUSE DEVELOPMENT

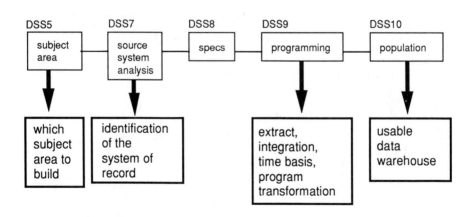

DSS5
subject area

DSS7
source system analysis

DSS8
specs

DSS9
programming

DSS10
population

which subject area to build

identification of the system of record

extract, integration, time basis, program transformation

usable data warehouse

The deliverable for source system analysis is the identification of the system of record for the subject area being considered. The deliverable for the programming phase is the programs that will extract, integrate, and change data from current value to time variant.

The final deliverable in the population of the data warehouse is the actual population of the warehouse. It is noted that the population of data into the warehouse is an ongoing activity.

Deliverables for the heuristic levels of processing are not as easy to define as they are for the operational and data warehouse levels of development. The heuristic nature of the analytical processing in this phase is much more informal. However, Figure METH 10 shows some of the deliverables associated with heuristic processing based on the data warehouse.

Figure METH 10 shows that data pulled from the warehouse is the result of the extraction program. The deliverable of the subsequent analysis step is further analysis based on data already refined. Finally, the deliverable of the final analysis of data is the satisfaction of (and understanding of) requirements.

METH 10

DELIVERABLES FOR THE HEURISTIC LEVEL OF PROCESSING

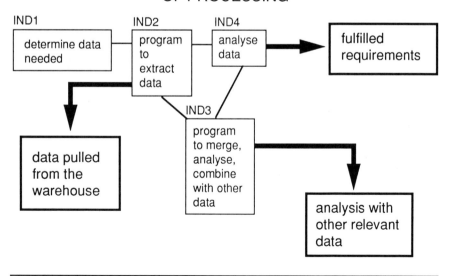

A Linear Flow of Deliverables

Except for heuristic processing, a linear flow of deliverables is to be expected. Figure METH 11 shows a sample of deliverables that would result from the execution of the process analysis component of the data-driven development methodology.

METH 11

A LINEAR FLOW OF DELIVERABLES FOR OPERATIONAL PROCESS ANALYSIS

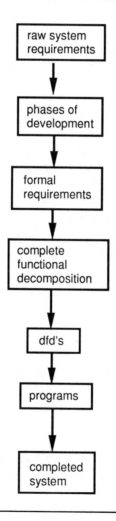

It is true that within reason there is a linear flow of deliverables. However, the linear flow shown glosses over two important aspects:

- The deliverables are usually produced in an iterative fashion.
- There are multiple deliverables at any given level. In other words, deliverables at any one level have the capability of spawning multiple deliverables at the next lower level, as shown by Figure METH 12.

Figure METH 12 shows that a single requirements definition results in three development phases. Each development phase goes through formal requirements definition and into decomposition. From the decomposition, multiple activities are identified, each of which has a dfd created for it. In turn, each dfd creates one or more programs. Ultimately, the programs form the backbone of the completed system.

Estimating Resources Required for Development

Looking at the diagram shown by Figure METH 12, it becomes apparent that once the specifics of exactly how many deliverables are being spawned is designed, then an estimation of how many resources the development process will take can be rationally done.

Figure METH 13 shows a simple technique.

In Figure METH 13, each level of deliverables first is defined so that the total number of deliverables is known. Then the time required for the building of each deliverable is multiplied by each deliverable, yielding an estimate of the manpower resources required.

SDLC/CLDS

Earlier discussions alluded to the fact that operational systems are built under one system development life cycle, and DSS systems are built under another system development life cycle. Figure METH 14 shows the development life cycle associated with operational systems.

In Figure METH 14, requirements are at the starting point. The next activities include analysis, design, programming, testing, integration, implementation, and maintenance.

METH 12

DELIVERABLES USUALLY SPAWN MULTIPLE
DELIVERABLE AT A LOWER LEVEL

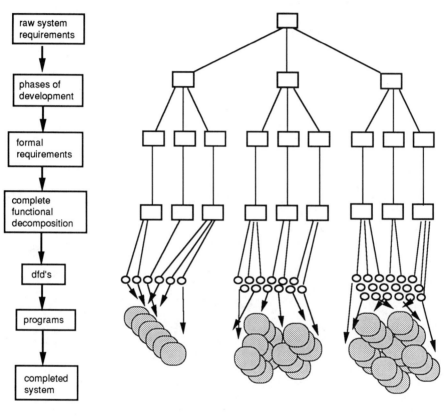

raw system requirements

phases of development

formal requirements

complete functional decomposition

dfd's

programs

completed system

METH 13

ESTIMATING SYSTEM DEVELOPMENT TIME

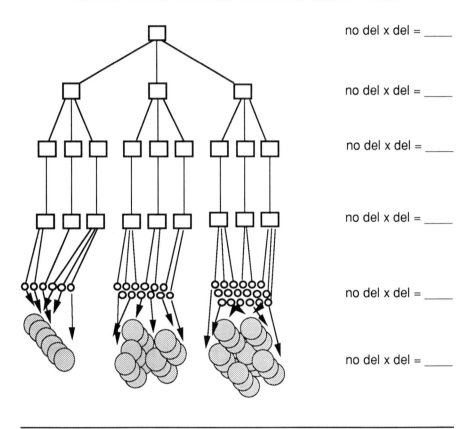

no del x del = ____

no del x del = ____

no del x del = ____

no del x del = ____

no del x del = ____

no del x del = ____

The system development life cycle associated with DSS systems is shown by Figure METH 15.

Figure METH 15 shows that DSS processing begins with data. Once data for analysis is secured (usually by using the data warehouse!), programming, analysis, and so forth continue. The development life cycle for DSS data ends with an understanding of the requirements of what is needed.

METH 14

the classical system development life cycle

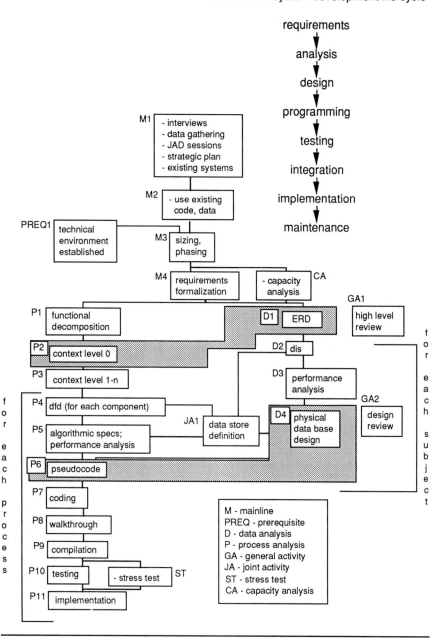

requirements
↓
analysis
↓
design
↓
programming
↓
testing
↓
integration
↓
implementation
↓
maintenance

M1 | - interviews
- data gathering
- JAD sessions
- strategic plan
- existing systems

M2 | - use existing code, data

PREQ1 | technical environment established

M3 | sizing, phasing

M4 | requirements formalization

CA | - capacity analysis

GA1 | high level review

P1 | functional decomposition

D1 | ERD

P2 | context level 0

D2 | dis

P3 | context level 1-n

D3 | performance analysis

GA2 | design review

P4 | dfd (for each component)

JA1 | data store definition

D4 | physical data base design

P5 | algorithmic specs; performance analysis

P6 | pseudocode

P7 | coding

P8 | walkthrough

P9 | compilation

P10 | testing

ST | - stress test

P11 | implementation

for each process

for each subject

M - mainline
PREQ - prerequisite
D - data analysis
P - process analysis
GA - general activity
JA - joint activity
ST - stress test
CA - capacity analysis

METH 15

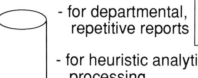

DEPT1

- for departmental, repetitive reports | standard requirements development for reports

- for heuristic analytical processing

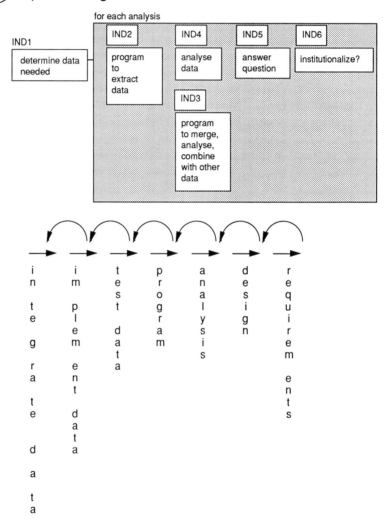

for each analysis

IND1

determine data needed

IND2

program to extract data

IND3

program to merge, analyse, combine with other data

IND4

analyse data

IND5

answer question

IND6

institutionalize?

integrate data → implement data → test data → program → analysis → design → requirements

Data Dictionary

The role of data dictionary is depicted by the graph shown in Figure METH 16.

Data dictionary plays a central role in operational processing in the activities of ERD development and documentation, dis development, physical database design, and coding. Data dictionary plays a heavy role in data model analysis, subject area selection, source system selection (system of record identification), and programming in the world of data warehouse development.

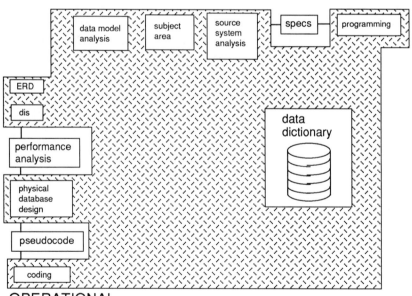

METH 16

DATA WAREHOUSE DEVELOPMENT

the role of data dictionary
in the development process
for data-driven development

What About Existing Systems?

In very few cases is development done freshly with no backlog of existing systems. Existing systems certainly present no problem to the DSS component of the data-driven development methodology. Finding the system of record in existing systems to serve as a basis for warehouse data is a normal event.

However, a word needs to be said about existing systems in the operational environment. The first approach to existing operational systems is to try to build on them. When this is possible, much productivity is the result. But in many cases existing operational systems cannot be built upon.

The second stance is to try to modify existing operational systems. In some cases this is a possibility; in most cases it is not possible.

The third stance is to do a wholesale replacement and enhancement of existing operational systems. In this case, the existing operational system serves as a basis for gathering requirements, and no more.

A variant of a wholesale replacement is the conversion of some or all of an existing operational system. This approach works on a limited basis, where the existing system is small and simple. The larger and more complex the existing operational system, the less likelihood that the system can be converted.

Glossary

access—the operation of seeking, reading, or writing data on a storage unit.

access method—a technique used to transfer a physical record from or to a mass storage device.

access pattern—the general sequence in which the data structure is accessed (for example, from tuple to tuple, from record to record, from segment to segment, etc.).

accuracy—a qualitative assessment of freedom from error or a quantitative measure of the magnitude of error, expressed as a function of relative error.

ad hoc processing—one time only, casual access, and manipulation of data on parameters never before used, usually done in a heuristic, iterative manner.

after image—the snapshot of data placed on a log upon the completion of a transaction.

agent of change—a motivating force large enough not to be denied, usually aging of systems, changes in technology, radical changes in requirements, etc.

algorithm—a set of statements organized to solve a problem in a finite number of steps.

analytical processing—using the computer to produce an analysis for management decision, usually involving trend analysis, drill down analysis, demographic analysis, profiling, etc.

application—a group of algorithms and data interlinked to support an organizational requirement.

application database—a collection of data organized to support a specific application.

archival database—a collection of data containing data of a historical nature. As a rule, archival data cannot be updated. Each unit of archival data is relevant to a moment in time, now passed.

artifact—a design technique used to represent referential integrity in the DSS environment.

atomic—(1) data stored in a data warehouse; (2) the lowest level of process analysis.

atomic database—a database made up of primarily atomic data; a data warehouse; a DSS foundation database.

atomic level data—data with the lowest level of granularity. Atomic level data sits in a data warehouse and is time variant (i.e., accurate as of some moment in time now passed).

attribute—a property that can assume values for entities or relationships. Entities can be assigned several attributes (for example, a tuple in a relationship consists of values). Some systems also allow relationships to have attributes as well.

audit trail—data that are available to trace activity, usually update activity.

backup—a file serving as a basis for the activity of backing up a database. Usually a snapshot of a database as of some previous moment in time.

batch—computer environment n which programs (usually long running, sequentially oriented) access data exclusively, and user interaction is not allowed while the activity is occurring.

batch environment—a sequentially dominated mode of processing; in batch, input is collected and stored for future, later processing. Once collected, the batch input is transacted sequentially against one or more databases.

before image—a snapshot of a record prior to update, usually placed on an activity log.

bit map—a specialized form of an index indicating the existence or nonexistence of a condition for a group of blocks or records. Bit maps are expensive to build and maintain but provide very fast comparison and access facilities.

blocking—the combining of two or more physical records so that they are physically located together. The result of their physical co-location is that they can be accessed and fetched by a single execution of a machine instruction.

cache—a buffer usually built and maintained at the device level. Retrieving data out of a cache is much quicker than retrieving data out of a cylinder.

cardinality (of a relation)—the number of tuples (i.e., rows) in a relation.

CASE—Computer Aided Software Engineering

checkpoint—an identified snapshot of the database or a point at which the transactions against the database have been frozen or have been quiesced.

checkpoint/restart—a means of restarting a program at some point other than the beginning—for example, when a failure or interruption has occurred. N checkpoints may be used at intervals throughout an application program. At each of those points, sufficient information is stored to permit the program to be restored to the moment in time the checkpoint has been taken.

"CLDS"—the facetiously named system development life cycle for analytical, DSS systems. CLDS is so named because in fact it is the reverse of the classical systems development life cycle—SDLC.

COBOL—Common Business Oriented Language—a computer language for the business world. A very common language.

column—a vertical table in which values are selected from the same domain. A row is made up of one or more columns.

commonality of data—similar or identical data that occurs in different applications or systems. The recognition and management of commonality of data is one of the foundations of conceptual and physical database design.

compaction—a technique for reducing the number of bits required to represent data without losing the content of the data. With compaction, repetitive data are represented very concisely.

condensation—the process of reducing the volume of data managed without reducing the logical consistency of the data. Condensation is essentially different from compaction.

contention—the condition that occurs when two or more programs try to access the same data at the same time.

continuous time span data—data organized so that a continuous definition of data over a span of time is represented by one or more records.

CPU—central processing unit.

CPU-bound—the state of processing in which the computer can produce no more output because the CPU portion of the processor is being used at 100 percent capacity. When the computer is CPU-bound, typically the memory and storage processing units are less than 100 percent utilized. With modern DBMS, it is much more likely that the computer be I/O-bound, rather than CPU-bound.

current value data—data whose accuracy is valid as of the moment of execution, as opposed to time variant data.

DASD—see direct access storage device.

data—a recording of facts, concepts, or instructions on a storage medium for communication, retrieval, and processing by automatic means and presentation as information that is understandable by human beings.

data administrator—(DA)—the individual or organization responsible for the specification, acquisition, and maintenance of data management software and the design, validation and security of files or databases. The data model and the data dictionary are classically the charge of the DA.

database—a collection of interrelated data stored (often with controlled, limited redundancy) according to a schema. A database can serve single or multiple applications.

database administrator (DBA)—the organizational function charged with the day-to-day monitoring and care of the databases. The DBA function is more closely associated with physical database design than the DA is.

database key—a unique value that exists for each record in a database. The value is often indexed, although it can be randomized or hashed.

database management system (DBMS)—a computer based software system used to establish and manage data.

data-driven development—the approach to development that centers around identifying the commonality of data through a data model and building programs that have a broader scope than the immediate application. Data-driven development differs from classical application-oriented development.

data element—(1) an attribute of an entity; (2) a uniquely named and well-defined category of data that consists of data items and that is included in a record of an activity.

data item set (dis)—a grouping of data items, each of which directly relates to the key of the grouping of data in which the data items reside. The data item set is found in the midlevel model.

data model—(1) the logical data structures, including operations and constraints provided by a DBMS for effective database processing; (2) the system used for the representation of data (for example, the ERD or relational model).

data structure—a logical relationship among data elements that is designed to support specific data manipulation functions (trees, lists, and tables).

data warehouse—a collection of integrated, subject-oriented databases designed to support the DSS function, where each unit of data is relevant to some moment in time. The data warehouse contains atomic data and lightly summarized data.

decision support system (DSS)—a system used to support managerial decisions. Usually DSS involves the analysis of many units of data in a heuristic fashion. As a rule, DSS processing does not involve the update of data.

decompaction—the opposite of compaction; once data is stored in a compacted form, it must be decompacted to be used.

denormalization—the technique of placing normalized data in a physical location that optimizes the performance of the system.

derived data—data whose existence depends on two or more occurrences of a major subject of the enterprise.

derived data element—a data element that is not necessarily stored but that can be generated when needed (age, current date, date of birth).

design review—the quality assurance process in which all aspects of a system are reviewed publicly prior to the striking of code.

direct access—retrieval or storage of data by reference to its location on a volume. The access mechanism goes directly to the data in question, as is generally required with online use of data. Also called random access or hashed access.

direct access storage device (DASD)—a data storage unit on which data can be accessed directly without having to progress through a serial file such as a magnetic tape file. A disk unit is a direct access storage device.

download—the stripping of data from one database to another based on the content of data found in the first database.

drill-down analysis—the type of analysis where examination of a summary number leads to the exploration of the components of the sum.

dual database—the practice of separating high-performance, transaction-oriented data from decision support data.

dual database management systems—the practice of using multiple database management systems to control different aspects of the database environment.

dumb terminal—a device used to interact directly with the end user where all processing is done on a remote computer. A dumb terminal acts as a device that gathers data and displays data only.

EIS (Executive Information Systems)—systems designed for the top executive, featuring drill-down analysis and trend analysis.

encoding—a shortening or abbreviation of the physical representation of a data value (e.g., male = "M," female = "F").

entity—a person, place, or thing of interest to the data modeller at the highest level of abstraction.

entity—relationship diagram (ERD)—a high-level data model— the schematic showing all the entities within the scope of integration and the direct relationship between those entities.

event—a signal that an activity of significance has occurred. An event is noted by the information system.

external data—(1) data originating from other than the operational systems of a corporation; (2) data residing outside the central processing complex.

extract—the process of selecting data from one environment and transporting it to another environment.

flat file—a collection of records containing no data aggregates, nested repeated data items, or groups of data items.

foreign key—an attribute that is not a primary key in a relational system but whose values are the values of the primary key of another relation.

fourth-generation language—language or technology designed to allow the end user unfettered access to data.

functional decomposition—the division of operations into hierarchical functions (activities) that form the basis for procedures.

granularity—the level of detail contained in a unit of data. The more detail there is, the lower the level of granularity. The less detail there is, the higher the level of granularity.

heuristic—the mode of analysis in which the next step is determined by the results of the current step of analysis. Used for decision support processing.

image copy—a procedure in which a database is physically copied to another medium for the purposes of backup.

index—the portion of the storage structure maintained to provide efficient access to a record when its index key item is known.

information—data that human beings assimilate and evaluate to solve a problem or make a decision.

integrity—the property of a database that ensures that the data contained in the database is as accurate and consistent as possible.

interactive—a mode of processing that combines some of the characteristics of online transaction processing and batch processing. In interactive processing, the end user interacts with data over which he/she has exclusive control. In addition, the end user can initiate background activity to be run against the data.

"is a type of"—an analytical tool used in abstracting data during the process of conceptual database design (for example, a cocker spaniel is a type of dog).

iterative analysis—the mode of processing in which the next step of processing depends on the results obtained by the existing step in execution; heuristic processing.

JAD (joint application design)—an organization of people— usually end users—to create and refine application system requirements.

judgment sample—a sample of data where data is accepted or rejected for the sample based on one or more parameters.

key—a data item or combination of data items used to identify or locate a record instance (or other similar data groupings).

key, primary—a unique attribute used to identify a single record in a database.

key, secondary—a nonunique attribute used to identify a class of records in a database.

living sample—a representative database typically used for heuristic, statistical, analytical processing in place of a large database. Periodically, the very large database is selectively stripped of data so that the resulting living sample database represents a cross section of the very large database as of some moment in time.

load—to insert data values into a database that was previously empty.

log—a journal of activity.

logging—the automatic recording of data with regard to the access of the data, the updates to the data, etc.

loss of identity—when data are brought in from an external source and the identity of the external source is discarded, loss of identity occurs. A common practice with microprocessor data.

magnetic tape—(1) the storage medium most closely associated with sequential processing; (2) a large ribbon on which magnetic images are stored and retrieved.

master file—a file that holds the system of record for a given set of data (usually bound by an application).

metadata—(1) data about data; (2) the description of the structure, content, keys, indexes, etc., of data.

microprocessor—a small processor serving the needs of a single user.

migration—the process by which frequently used items of data are moved to more readily accessible areas of storage and infrequently used items of data are moved to less readily accessible areas of storage.

mips (million instructions per second)—the standard measurement of processor speed for minicomputers and mainframe computers.

online storage—storage devices and storage medium where data can be accessed in a direct fashion.

operational data—data used to support the daily processing a company does.

operations—the department charged with the running of the computer.

optical disk—a storage medium using lasers as opposed to magnetic devices. Optical disk is typically write only, is much less expensive per byte than magnetic storage, and is highly reliable.

overflow—(1) the condition in which a record or a segment cannot be stored in its home address because the address is already occupied. In this case, the data is placed in another location referred to as overflow. (2) the area of DASD where data is sent when the overflow condition is triggered.

ownership—the responsibility for updating operational data.

page—(1) a basic unit of data on DASD; (2) a basic unit of storage in main memory.

parameter—an elementary data value used as a criteria for qualification, usually of data searches or in the control of modules.

partition—a segmentation technique in which data are divided into physically different units. Partitioning can be done at the application or the system level.

populate—to place occurrences of data values in a previously empty database. See **load**.

primary key—an attribute that contains values that uniquely identify the record in which the key exists.

primitive data—data whose existence depends on only a single occurrence of a major subject area of the enterprise.

processor—the hardware at the center of execution of computer programs. Generally speaking, processors are divided into three categories—mainframes, minicomputers, and microcomputers.

processor cycles—the hardware's internal cycles that drive the computer (e.g., initiate I/O, perform logic, move data, perform arithmetic functions).

production environment—the environment where operational, high-performance processing is run.

punched cards—an early storage medium on which data and input were stored. Today punched cards are rare.

query language—a language that enables an end user to interact directly with a DBMS to retrieve and possibly modify data held under the DBMS.

record—an aggregation of values of data organized by their relation to a common key.

record at a time processing—the access of data record at a time, a tuple at a time, etc.

recovery—the restoration of the database to an original position or condition, often after major damage to the physical medium. See rollback and/or commit.

redundancy—the practice of storing more than one occurrence of data. In the case where data can be updated, redundancy poses serious problems. In the case where data is not updated, redundancy is often a valuable and necessary design technique.

referential integrity—the facility of a DBMS to ensure the validity of predefined relationships.

reorganization—the process of unloading data in a poorly organized state and reloading the data in a well-organized state.

Reorganization in some DBMS is used to restructure data. Often reorganization is called "reorg." Often called an "unload/reload" process.

repeating groups—a collection of data that can occur several times within a given record occurrence.

rolling summary—a form of storing archival data where the most recent data has the most details stored, and data that is older has fewer details stored.

scope of integration—the formal definition of what the boundaries of the system being modeled are and are not.

SDLC—System Development Life Cycle—the classical operational system development life cycle that typically includes requirements gathering, analysis, design, programming, testing, integration, and implementation.

sequential file—a file in which records are ordered according to the values of one or more key fields. The records can be processed in this sequence starting from the first record in the file, continuing to the last record in the file.

serial file—a sequential file in which the records are physically adjacent, in sequential order.

set at a time processing—access of data by groups, each member of which satisfies a selection criterion.

snapshot—a database dump or the archival of data out of a database as of some moment in time.

solutions database—the component of a DSS environment where the results of previous decisions are stored. Solutions databases are consulted to help determine the proper course of action in a current decision-making situation.

storage hierarchy—storage units linked to form a storage subsystem, in which some units are fast but small and expensive, and other units are large but slower and less expensive.

subject database—a database organized around a major subject of the corporation. Classical subject databases are for customer, transaction, product, part, vendor.

system log—an audit trail of relevant system events (for example, transaction entries, database changes, etc.)

system of record—the definitive and singular source of operational data. If data element abc has a value of 25 in one database record and a value of 45 in the system of record, by definition, the first value is incorrect and must be reconciled. The system of record is useful for managing redundancy of data.

table—a relation that consists of a set of columns with a heading and a set of rows (i.e., tuples).

time stamping—the practice of tagging each record with some moment in time, usually when the record was created or when the record was passed from one environment to another.

time variant data—data whose accuracy is relevant to some moment in time. The three forms of time variant data are continuous time span, event discrete, and periodic discrete data. See current value data.

transition data—data possessing both primitive and derived characteristics; usually very sensitive to the running of the business. Typical transition data are interest rates for a bank, policy rates for an insurance company, retail sale rates for a manufacturer/distributor, etc.

trend analysis—the process of looking at homogeneous data over a spectrum of time. See EIS.

true archival data—data at the lowest level in the atomic database, usually stored on bulk storage.

update—to change, add, delete, or replace values in all or selected entries, groups, or attributes stored in a database.

user—a person or process issuing commands and messages to the information system.

References

Boehm, B. *Software Engineering Economics*, Prentice-Hall, Englewood Cliffs, NJ, 1981.

Brooks, F. P., Jr. *The Mythical Manmonth: Essays on Software Engineering*, Addison-Wesley, Reading, MA, 1974.

Chen, P. P. "The Entity Relationship Model—Toward a Unified View Of Data," in *Transactions on Database Systems*, Vol. 1, No. 1, March 1976.

——. *The Entity Relationship Approach to Logical Database Design*, QED Info Sciences, Wellesley, MA, 1977.

Date, C. J. *An Introduction to Database Systems*, Addison-Wesley, Reading, MA, 1975.

Davis, A. M. "Automating the Requirements Phase: Benefits to Later Phases of Software Life Cycle," in *COMPSAC 80, Proceedings IEEE*, Computer Society, Los Alamitos, CA, October 1980.

Davis G. B., and M. H. Olson. "Developing a Long-Range Information Systems Plan in Management Information Systems," McGraw Hill, New York, 1985.

DeMarco, T. Structured Analysis and Systems Specification, Yourdon Press, New York, 1978.

Digital Equipment Corporation manual, *Information Systems Technical Strategy and Architecture*, DEC, Marlboro, MA, June 1989.

Gane, C., and T. Sarson. *Structured Systems Analysis: Tools and Techniques*, Prentice-Hall Englewood Cliffs, NJ, 1979.

Inmon, W. H. *Information Engineering for the Practitioner*, Yourdon Press, New York, 1988.

———. *Using DB2 for Decision Support Systems*, QED, Wellesley, MA, 1989.

———. *Using Oracle for Decision Support Systems*, QED, Wellesley, MA, 1989.

———. *Third Wave Processing: Data Base Machines and Decision Support Systems*, QED, Wellesley, MA, 1991.

———. *Using Rdb for Decision Support Systems*, QED, Wellesley, MA, 1992.

———. *Understanding Data Pattern Processing*, QED, Wellesley, MA, 1991 (with S Osterfelt).

———. *Practical Information Engineering*, QED, Wellesley, MA, 1992.

Jackson, M. A. *Principles of Program Design*, Academic Press, NY, 1975.

Karimi, J. "Computer Aided Process Organization in Software Design," Dept. of MIS, University of Arizona, 1983.

Kerr, M. J. *The IRM Imperative*, John Wiley Press, New York, 1990.

Konsynski, B. R., and R. J. Nunamaker. *Decision Support in Enterprise Analysis*, Plenum Publishing, NY, 1984.

Loper, M., and W. H. Inmon. "A Unified Data Architecture for Systems Integration," ISEC Conference, Washington, DC (Feb).

Martin, J. *Strategic Data Planning Methodologies*, Prentice-Hall, Englewood Cliffs, NJ, 1982.

Martin, J., and C. Finklestein. *Information Engineering*, Savant Institute, Cornforth, Lancashire, England, 1981.

Meyer, D., and M. Boone. *The Information Edge*, Dow Jones Irwin, Homewood, IL, 1988.

Orr, K. T. *Structured Systems Development*, Yourdon Press, NY, 1977.

Parker, M., R. Benson, and E. Trainor. Information Economics: Linking Business Performance to Information Technology, Prentice-Hall, Englewood Cliffs, NJ, 1989.

Perkinson, R. *Data Analysis: The Key to Database Design*, QED, Wellesley, MA, 1984.

Rousopolous, N. "The Logical Access Path Schema of a Database Design," ACM Transactions in Software Engineering, Vol. SE-8, No. 6, November 1982.

Smith, J. M., and D. C. P. Smith. "Conceptual Database Design," INFOTECH, State of the Art Report on Database Design, June 1978.

———. "Database Abstraction Aggregation," Communications of the ACM, Vol. 20, No. 6, June 1977.

Teichrow, D., and E. A. Hershey. "PSL/PSA: A Computer Aided Technique for Structured Documentation and Analysis of Information Processing Systems," in *IEEE Transactions on Software Engineering*, Vol. SE-3, No. 1, 1977.

Tschritzis, D. C., and F. H. Lochovsky. *Data Models*, Prentice-Hall, Englewood Cliffs, NJ, 1981.

Yourdon, E. *Techniques of Program Structure and Design*, Prentice-Hall, Englewood Cliffs, NJ, 1975.

Zachman, J. "A Framework for Information Systems Architecture," *IBM Systems Journal*, Vol. 26, No. 3, White Plains, NY, 1986.

Index

4GL, 4, 5
24-hour time delay, 170

A

Accurate, 166
Action item, 184
Addressability, 107
Agents of change, 174
Aging, 174
Algorithm, 84
Algorithmic differential, 8, 9, 91
Alterations, 189
Analytical processing, 30
Appendix, 163, 175, 177
Application, 61, 62
   -by-application, 177
   code, 46
   level, 46, 47
   programming, 194
Appraisal, 184
Architected environment, 25, 132
Architecture, 63, 145, 163, 174

Archival, 192, 197
Array, 193
   of data, 80, 81, 166
Artifacts, 67, 86, 88, 166, 193
   of data, 194
Atomic, 18
Attribute, 71, 73, 80, 164, 186, 187
Audit, 62
   requirements, 196
Auditing, 53, 54, 185
Availability agreement, 191
Available remaining space, 110
Average day, 191

B

Back flows, 199
Backup, 54
Bank teller systems, 4
Batch window, 181
Before and after image, 63, 188
Bias, 43

265